(*continued on back*)

TOWARD A NEW PERSONOLOGY

TOWARD A NEW PERSONOLOGY

An Evolutionary Model

Theodore Millon

WILEY

John Wiley & Sons, Inc.

New York · Chichester · Brisbane ·
Toronto · Singapore

To the Memory of

GARDNER MURPHY

and

HENRY A. MURRAY

for the Open and Creative Spirit with which
they Endowed their Students

Library of Congress Cataloging-in-Publication Data
Millon, Theodore.
   Toward a new personology: an evolutionary model / Theodore Millon.
      p.   cm. -- (Wiley series on personality processes)
   Includes bibliographical references.
   ISBN 0-471-51573-6
   1. Personality.   2. Personality development.   3. Personality disorders.   4. Genetic psychology.   I. Title.   II. Series.
BF698.M552   1990
616.89--dc20   89-35944
                                                                    CIP

Printed in the United States of America
90 91 10 9 8 7 6 5 4 3 2 1

SERIES PREFACE

This series of books is addressed to behavioral scientists interested in the nature of human personality. Its scope should prove pertinent to personality theorists and researchers as well as to clinicians concerned with applying an understanding of personality processes to the amelioration of emotional difficulties in living. To this end, the series provides a scholarly integration of theoretical formulations, empirical data, and practical recommendations.

Six major aspects of studying and learning about human personality can be designated: personality theory, personality structure and dynamics, personality development, personality assessment, personality change, and personality adjustment. In exploring these aspects of personality, the books in the series discuss a number of distinct but related subject areas: the nature and implications of various theories of personality; personality characteristics that account for consistencies and variations in human behavior; the emergence of personality processes in children and adolescents; the use of interviewing and testing procedures to evaluate individual differences in personality; efforts to modify personality styles through psychotherapy, counseling, behavior therapy, and other methods of influence; and patterns of abnormal personality functioning that impair individual competence.

IRVING B. WEINER

University of South Florida
Tampa, Florida

CONTENTS

PROLOGUE

Historical Reflections

The reader may find it useful to know a few of the sources which inspired the author to write this text. Most significant has been the opportunity to participate in the recent renaissance of personology. Trends which previously led to a decline in studies of personality and its disorders have sharply reversed; personologic themes and issues that were given short shrift in the 1960s and 1970s have not only reemerged, but have moved into the limelight of clinical work. As written elsewhere (Millon, 1984), the long drought is over and a revival of the rich heritage of the 1940s and 1950s is underway. For some 30 years now, the enthusiasm that once characterized adherence to one or another personality theory, as well as faith in this or that personality instrument, has been buffeted by trivial, as well as just, criticisms. Additionally, the passage of time and the aging of once preeminent ideas and techniques have led not only to a creeping ennui, but also to the value schisms that inevitably separate generations. Hence, the marvelous theories (e. g., Lewin, Murray, Murphy, Sullivan) and incisive methods (e. g., Rorschach, TAT, Bender-Gestalt, figure drawing) of yesteryear have faded inexorably, or so it appears,

1

to a status more benefiting quaint historic notions and intriguing, albeit ancient, tools.

Were the powers that once enabled comprehensive and valid personality assessments a fantasy of the past, impertinent, if not grandiose, acts by a then immature and arrogant young science? Were the personality theories then espoused equally ill-considered, presumptuous aspirations of ill-informed and naive, if not cavalier, speculators who asserted knowledge to themselves far greater than "the facts" would warrant?

What were once the splendidly astute and discriminating clinical portrayals by Freud, Reich, and Horney, each of whom stirred our curiosities and inspired us to further our desire to know, had become outdated curiosities, grandiose speculations to be replaced by tightly focused and empirically anchored constructs. The conceptual models and cogent insights of Freud, Jung, and Adler resonated with our early, personally more prosaic efforts to penetrate and give order to the mysteries of patients' psychic worlds, but they too were out of vogue, skillfully rent by what can be termed the anticoherency and anticonsistency movements. No longer was personality to be seen as an integrated gestalt, a dynamic system comprising more than the mere sum of its parts. The pendulum swung toward empiricism and positivism; only "observable" facts were in the ascendancy. The personality configuration was segmented into its ostensive constituents, construed as stimulus-response (S-R) bonds by some, statistical factors by others, dimensional traits elsewhere, and so on. This loose, anticoherency amalgam, however divergent its members may have been on other scores—and they were quite vociferous about *their* disagreements—did agree on one matter—that personality was best disassembled, arranged in one set of component parts or another. Given that most were nomothetically, rather than idiographically inclined, this new breed of quasi-empiricist made a shambles of the inspired "personality-as-a-coherent-whole" theories which nurtured those who entered the clinical field in the post-World War II era.

Adding insult to the segmenting injuries of the anti-coherency movement was the clever, if not cynical, assault of the anticonsistency group. This egregious attack was based on a facile and highly selective reading of the research literature, a reading so biased in its choices and interpretations that it justifies the very denunciations its promulgators employed themselves in condemning personality concepts such as disposition, stability, and generality. Widely read, printed and re-printed in every text, as well as blandly (blindly?) accepted by journal editors as factually grounded, these critiques challenged the very foundations of the personality construct, no less its assessment. Comparable in several respects to earlier, adroit "decimations" of the efficacy of psychotherapy, those comprising the anticonsistency movement boldly confronted believers in any and all personality theories with an ostensively impeccable evidential base for the insubstantiality of these sentiments. And, with the empirical grounding of personality in question, with the very logic of intrapsychic coherence and behavioral consistency under attack, adherents and proponents of an integrative or holistic view of personality not only withdrew from open display, tails properly tucked, but were driven both from texts and journals, losing their once vaunted academic respectability and shamed should they publicly exhibit their archaic and "unscientific" beliefs.

The 1960s and 1970s were difficult times indeed. Of all the favored tools and ideas of an earlier epoch, the projective techniques and psychoanalytic theory were hit hardest. Perhaps most serious of all, however, was the slow but inexorable loss of the intellectually curious, abstractly philosophical, and ambiguity-tolerant student, the kind that had been turned on by the very intangibles of "mind," those intuitively sensed, yet ever obscure and difficult-to-fathom processes which sustained and gave coherence to the observable world. Both psychiatry and psychology suffered this loss, and for similar reasons. Emotionally attuned medical students were attracted in the 1940s and 1950s to the psychoanalytic orientation then characterizing psychiatry. Similarly, graduate students drawn to the dynamics of a recondite intrapsychic world were intrigued by opportunities to study it via the new and fascinating projective methods. Over the decades, however, analytic theory and projective assessment came under severe attacks, being judged either or both unscientific and socially irrelevant. The community mental health movement soon took hold in the 1960s and early 1970s, followed closely and concurrently by clinical behaviorism in psychology and clinical biochemistry in psychiatry. And with these movements the character of incoming students began to change. "Intellectual types" who were attracted by the inscrutable and intangible, stirred by abstruse unknowns and the enigmatic, no longer found the field quite as intriguing as in earlier days. Consonant with the character of the decade, the 1960s solicited the socially committed, the student who saw psychology and psychiatry as vehicles to change an unjust society. Worthy though such aspirations may have been, they drew a different breed of students. Although different in outlook, these new recruits were among the most able students seeking careers in line with idealistic social goals. Quality remained high, but of a different character as mental health expanded its frontiers beyond the inner recesses of the patient's private world. The student body took its next and sharpest turn when the seductions of "scientism" were proferred in the guise of clinical behaviorism and psychiatric biochemistry. No longer were the two primary professions of mental health oriented to attract the intellectually reflective or the socially idealistic; they set out to entice anew those seeking ennoblement via scientific rigor and empiricism, the tangible and the "objectively real."

A change in the fortunes of personology was brewing through the 1970s. Slow though this awakening may have been, there were signs of emerging new ideas and challenges that gave promise of reviving the luster of the 1940s and 1950s. By virtue of time, reflection and, not the least, of a growing disenchantment with available alternatives, evident notably in significant reappraisals among its most fevered critics, the

place of personality as a construct began to regain its formerly
solid footing.

Especially promising was the observation that the essential element that gave substance to "personality" as construct
—the fact that people exhibit distinctive and abiding characteristics—has reemerged, despite the early attacks of anticonsistency and anticoherency critics. This durability attests, at
the very least, to its intuitive consonance with authentic observation, a viability all the more noteworthy when one considers
the spirited, if misguided, academic efforts to undo it. This
renaissance is particularly impressive when one considers the
vast number of recently popular constructs that have faded to a
status consonant with their trivial character, or have suc-
cumbed, under the weight of their scientific inefficacy, to
scholarly boredom.

Personality theory appears to have weathered its mettle-
some assaults. Witness the changing views of its most ardent
critics; moreover, it seems to be undergoing a wide-ranging
resurgence. Notable here are the widely acclaimed formulations
of contemporary analytic theorists, particularly Kernberg
(1975) and Kohut (1971). No less significant in this realm are
theoretical ideas posited by a reactivated interpersonal school,
led by such post-Sullivan and post-Leary theorists as Benjamin
(1984), Wiggins (1982), and Kiesler (1986). Of perhaps even
greater note, though not necessarily in the substantive merit of
their proposals, but rather in the striking shift their ideas have
taken from their former anticonsistency and anticoherency
position, are the recent "ecumenical" formulations of social
learning theorists such as Bandura (1977) and Mischel (1984).
Shedding an earlier behavioristic dogmatism and no longer
assigning primacy to situational determinants, these theorists
have "reconnected" behaviorism to cognitivism, asserting not
only an intrinsic coherence between them, but proclaiming
that generalities do exist among psychic functions as a consequence of the coordinating effects of cognitive processes. As the
inherent unity of personality regains its former standing and

becomes increasingly fashionable, perhaps its erstwhile adversaries will soon "discover" the merits of a psychoanalytic-cognitive-behavioral synthesis of psychological functions, as well as promulgate the efficacy of parallel "multidimensional" approaches to treatment. How interesting it is that those who led the anticonsistency and anticoherency effort in the 1960s to bury personology as a discipline are now moving subtly to the forefront in its resuscitation.

The revival of personology as central to the clinical enterprise arises from other, more practical considerations. For example, most mental health practitioners employ their professional skills today in outpatient rather than in-patient settings. Their "clients" are no longer the severely disturbed "State Hospital" psychotic, but ambulatory individuals seen in office settings or community clinics, beset with personal stressors, social inadequacies, or interpersonal conflicts, typically reported in symptoms such as anxiety, depression, or alcoholism, but which signify the outcroppings of longstanding and deeply ingrained patterns of maladaptive behaving, feeling, thinking, and relating: in other words, their "personality style."

It is not only the changing patient population of clinical practice, or the emergence of attractively new personologic theories from refurbished analytic, interpersonal or social learning perspectives, or even advances in the realm of quantitative assessment and psychometrics that signify the growing prominence of the construct. The very special status assigned the personality syndromes in the *DSM-III* (American Psychiatric Association, 1980) was both a reflection of these changes and instrumental in their further enhancement. With the advent of this official classification, personality disorders not only gained a place of consequence among syndromal categories, but became central to its multiaxial schema. The logic for assigning personality its own axis is more than a matter of differentiating syndromes of a more acute and dramatic form from those of a longstanding and prosaic character. More relevant to this partitioning decision was the assertion that personality can serve usefully as a dynamic substrate from which clinicians can better grasp the significance and meaning of their patients' transient and florid disorders. In the *DSM-III*, then, personality disorders not only attained an nosological status of prominence in their own right, but were assigned a contextual role that made them fundamental to the understanding and interpretation of other psychopathologies.

Promising new theories, the special role assigned these disorders in the multiaxial system of the *DSM-III*, as well as the forthcoming ICD-10 and *DSM-IV*, all point to the growing clinical importance of personologic syndromes. The organization of the International Society for the Study of Personality Disorders in 1988, the initial publication of the *Journal of Personality Disorders* in 1987, and the cosponsorship of an International Congress on the Personality Disorders by the World Psychiatric Association in 1988 added further to the status and cross-cultural importance of personology as a science.

It is a time of rapid scientific and clinical advances, a time that seems propitious for ventures designed to bridge new ideas and syntheses. The intersection between the study of "psychopathology" and the study of "personality" is one of these spheres of significant intellectual activity and clinical responsibility. Theoretical formulations that bridge this intersection would represent a major and valued conceptual step, but to limit efforts to this junction alone will lead to overlooking the solid footings necessary for fundamental progress, and which are provided increasingly by more mature sciences (e.g., physics and evolutionary biology). By failing to coordinate propositions and constructs to principles and laws established in these advanced disciplines, psychological science will continue to float, so to speak, at its current level, an act that will ensure the need to return to this task another day.

The goal of this book is to connect the conceptual structure of personology to its foundations in the natural sciences. What is proposed herein is akin to Freud's abandoned *Project for a Scientific Psychology* (1895) and Wilson's highly controversial *Sociobiology* (1975). Both were worthy endeavors to advance our understanding of human nature; this was to be done by exploring interconnections among disciplines that evolved ostensibly unrelated bodies of research and manifestly dissimilar languages.

The proximal stimulus for writing these ideas was an invitation to deliver a lecture in honor of Henry A. Murray. Attempts to crystallize these thoughts often led me to the far-ranging speculations of another revered mentor, Gardner Murphy, a peer and friend of Murray's. The breadth of knowledge and imaginative spirit these two men shared emboldened me to stretch my thoughts beyond what would have been the merely pedestrian. It is to them that I have dedicated this book. What is substantive and creative within it owes much to their inspiration; the author bears full responsibility for what is sterile and mere presumption.

Two others, even more central to my development, deserve mention as having provided both the motivation and orientation that characterizes the theoretical model to be presented. From earliest childhood, I have struggled with polarities either within myself or between others. On one side of my ancestry, I observed my mother, swept by her recurrent moods, acting in response to her heart; on the other, my father, though warm and loving, believing that only the logic of mind could bring about life's solutions. To master these contrasting elements of my nature, and to construct cohesion where perhaps none existed became the driving force of both my personal and professional life, an orientation whose chief aim appears to have been the integration of what others have viewed as unconnected, if not divergent. Whether my "integrative" efforts are merely symbolic attempts to construct an inner coherence to self is not for me to judge. Readers can gauge the validity of one such endeavor as they contemplate the chapters that follow.

CHAPTER ONE

INTRODUCTION

On Scientific Creativity and Theoretical Integration

*E*specially *for human beings, life is a continuous procession of explorations, surmises, hunches, guesses, and experiments, failures and successes, of learnings and relearnings (Murray, 1959).*

Putting aside the highly seminal *Personality* (Murphy, 1947) and *Explorations* (Murray, 1938) volumes, for which they were known best among contemporary psychologists, Murphy and Murray were at heart speculative organizers of the mind, explorers who sifted through the chaos they came upon, searching for ways to create an aesthetic order, a simplified schema that would identify essences to replace the potpourri of incidentals they viewed as littering the fields of their inquiry. Challenging established assumptions and looking for the unexpected, they thrived on novelty, enjoyed ambiguity, and cast about for a "scaffolding" that might cage the zoo of needs and presses they had enumerated. As evident by the scope and diversity of their pursuits, they lived both the rational and the intuitive, enacting through their life's work Einstein's observation that science and art are branches of the same tree.

How can we best honor the indomitable spirit of creativity that characterized the almost 100 years that each of these men lived? This can be done most wisely by breaking free of the compulsively insecure empiricism that has narrowed this past generation's vision, becoming open once more to imaginative speculations, even of the most tenuous kind.

Unfortunately, the "grand" psychological theories of the 1920s and 1930s failed to fulfill their promise, resulting in few unifying proposals these past decades. What confidence that integrative schemas in realms such as personality or learning could be fashioned by the convergence of a few basic psychological variables gave way as a feasible aspiration by the 1960s. A hesitant conservatism, either antitheoretical or proempirical in character, gained sway, illustrated in personality by the growth of what was referred to in the Prologue as the anticonsistency and anticoherency movements. What began haltingly has been a slow reemergence of the integrative mindset, tentative proposals of an "ecumenical" nature that seek to bridge diverse psychological methods and processes. The dislodging of behavioral concretism, the rebirth of cognitive science, and the growth of therapeutic eclecticism, illustrate this encouraging shift.

It is necessary to go beyond current conceptual boundaries, more specifically to explore carefully reasoned, as well as "intuitive" hypotheses that draw their principles, if not their substance, from more established, "adjacent" sciences. Not only may such steps bear new conceptual fruits, but they may provide a foundation that can undergird and guide our own discipline's explorations. Much of personology, no less psychology as a whole, remains adrift, divorced from broader spheres of scientific knowledge, isolated from firmly grounded, if not universal principles, leading one to continue building the patchwork quilt of concepts and data domains that characterize the field. Preoccupied with but a small part of the larger puzzle, or fearing accusations of reductionism, many fail thereby to draw on the rich possibilities to be found in other realms of scholarly pursuit. With few exceptions, cohering concepts that would connect this subject to those of its sister sciences have not been developed.

Despite the current profusion of new terminology, personology appears not to have advanced appreciably beyond Murphy's *Personality* and Murray's *Explorations*. We seem trapped in (obsessed with?) horizontal refinements. A search for integrative schemas and cohesive constructs that link its seekers closely to relevant observations and laws developed in more advanced fields is needed. The goal—albeit a rather "grandiose" one—is to refashion the patchwork quilt into a well-tailored and aesthetic tapestry that interweaves the diverse forms in which nature expresses itself.

And what better sphere is there within the psychological sciences to undertake such syntheses than with the subject matter of personology. Persons are the only organically integrated system in the psychological domain, evolved through the millennia and inherently created from birth as natural entities, rather than culture-bound and experience-derived gestalts. The intrinsic cohesion of persons is not merely a rhetorical construction, but an authentic substantive unity. Personologic features may often be dissonant, and may be partitioned conceptually for pragmatic or scientific purposes, but they are segments of an inseparable biopsychosocial entity.

To take this view is not to argue that different spheres of scientific inquiry should be equated, nor is it to seek a single, overarching conceptual system encompassing biology, psychology and sociology (Millon, 1983). Arguing in favor of establishing explicit links between these domains calls neither for a reductionistic philosophy, a belief in substantive identicality, or efforts to so fashion them by formal logic. Rather, one should aspire to their substantive concordance, empirical consistency, conceptual interfacing, convergent dialogues, and mutual enlightenment.

Integrative consonance such as described is not an aspiration limited to ostensibly diverse sciences, but is a worthy goal within the domains of each science. Particularly relevant in this regard are efforts that seek to coordinate the often separate realms that comprise a clinical science, namely: its theories, the classification system it has formulated, the diagnostic tools it employs, and the therapeutic techniques it implements. Rather than developing independently and being left to stand as autonomous and largely unconnected functions, a truly mature clinical science will embody explicit: (1) *theories*, that is, explanatory and heuristic conceptual schemas that are consistent with established knowledge in both its own and related sciences, and from which reasonably accurate propositions concerning pathological conditions can be both deduced and understood, enabling thereby the development of a formal (2) *nosology*, that is, a taxonomic classification of disorders that has been derived logically *from the theory*, and is arranged to provide a cohesive organization within which its major categories can readily be grouped and differentiated, permitting thereby the development of coordinated (3) *instruments*, that is, tools that are empirically grounded and sufficiently sensitive quantitatively to enable the theory's propositions and hypotheses to be adequately investigated and evaluated, and the categories comprising its nosology to be readily identified (diagnosed) and measured (dimensionalized), specifying therefrom target areas for (4) *interventions*, that is, strategies and techniques of therapy, designed in accord with the theory and oriented to modify problematic clinical characteristics consonant with professional standards and social responsibilities.

The following chapters are sequenced to follow the four elements that comprise a coordinated clinical science. Primary attention will be given in the next two chapters to the first of these, that of theory. The substantive principles to be presented draw heavily in both their inspiration and content from contemporary thought in physics and evolutionary biology.

A few words should be said at the outset concerning the undergirding framework used to structure the personology model. Bipolar or dimensional schemas are almost universally present in the literature; the earliest may be traced to ancient Eastern religions, most notably the Chinese *I Ching* texts and the Hebrews' *Kabala*. More modern, though equally speculative bipolar systems have been proposed by keen and broadly informed observers, such as Sigmund Freud and Carl Jung, or by empirically well-grounded and dimensionally oriented methodologists, such as Raymond Cattell and Hans Eysenck. Each of their proposals fascinate either by virtue of their intriguing portrayals or by the compelling power of their "data" or logic. For me, however, all failed in their quest for the ultimate character of human nature in that their conceptions float, so to speak, above the foundations built by contemporary physical and biological sciences. Formulas of a psychological nature must not only coordinate with, but be anchored firmly to observations derived specifically from modern principles of physical and biological evolution. It is on these underpinnings of knowledge that the polarity model presented in the following chapters has been grounded, and from which a deeper and clearer understanding may be obtained concerning the nature of both normal and pathological functioning.

Nevertheless, what follows remains conjectural, if not overly extended in its speculative reach. In essence, it seeks to explicate the structure and styles of personality with reference to deficient, imbalanced, or conflicted modes of ecologic adaptation and reproductive strategy. Some readers will judge these conjectures persuasive; a few will consider them "interesting," but essentially unconfirmable; still others will find little of merit in them. Whatever one's appraisal, the theoretical model that follows may best be approached in the spirit in which it was formulated—an effort to bring together observations from different domains of science in the hope that principles derived in adjacent fields can lead to a clearer understanding of their neighbors.

On the Utility of Theory

It was Kurt Lewin (1936) who wrote some 50 years ago that "there is nothing so practical as a good theory." Theory, when properly fashioned, ultimately provides more simplicity and clarity than unintegrated and scattered information. Unrelated knowledge and techniques, especially those based on surface similarities, are a sign of a primitive science, as has been effectively argued by contemporary philosophers of science (Hempel, 1961; Quine, 1961).

All natural sciences have organizing principles that not only create order but also provide the basis for generating hypotheses and stimulating new knowledge. A good theory not only summarizes and incorporates extant knowledge, but is heuristic, that is, has "systematic import," as Hempel has phrased it, in that it originates and develops new observations and new methods.

It is unfortunate that the number of theories that have been advanced to "explain" personality and its disorders is directly proportional to the internecine squabbling found in the literature. Paroxysms of "scientific virtue" and pieties of "methodological purity" rarely are exclaimed by theorists themselves, but by their less creative disciples. As I previously commented (Millon, 1969):

Theories arise typically from the perceptive observation and imaginative speculation of a creative scientist. This innovator is usually quite aware of the limits and deficiencies of his "invention" and is disposed in the early stages of his speculation to modify it as he develops new observations and insights. Unfortunately, after its utility has been proven in a modest and limited way, the theory frequently acquires a specious stature. Having clarified certain ambiguities and survived initial criticisms, it begins to accumulate a coterie of disciples. These less creative thinkers tend to accept the theory wholeheartedly and espouse its superior explanatory powers and terminology throughout the scientific market place. They hold to its propositions tenaciously and defend it blindly and unequivocally against opposition. In time it becomes a rigid and sacred dogma and, as a result, authority replaces the test of utility and empirical validity. Intelligent men become religious disciples; their theory is a doctrine of "truth," not a guide to the unknown (p. 41).

Ostensibly toward the end of pragmatic sobriety, those of an antitheory bias have sought to persuade the profession of the failings of premature formalization, warning that one cannot arrive at the desired future by lifting science by its own bootstraps. To them, there is no way to traverse the road other sciences have traveled without paying the dues of an arduous program of empirical research. Formalized axiomatics, they say, must await the accumulation of "hard" evidence that is simply not yet in. Shortcutting the route with ill-timed systematics will lead down primrose paths, preoccupying attentions as one wends fruitlessly through endless detours, each of which could be averted by holding fast to an empiricist philosophy and methodology.

No one argues against the view that theories that float, so to speak, on their own, unconcerned with the empirical domain should be seen as the fatuous achievements they are and the travesty they make of the virtues of a truly coherent conceptual system. Formal theory should not be "pushed" far beyond the data, and its derivations should be linked at all points to established observations. However, a theoretical framework can be a compelling instrument for coordinating and giving consonance to complex and diverse observations—if its concepts are linked to relevant facts in the empirical world. By probing "beneath" surface impressions to inner structures and processes, previously isolated facts and difficult to fathom data may yield new relationships and expose clearer meanings. Paul Meehl has noted (1978) that theoretical systems comprise related assertions, shared terms, and coordinated propositions that provide fertile grounds for deducing and deriving new empirical and clinical observations. Scientific progress occurs, then, when observations and concepts elaborate and refine previous work. However, this progression does not advance by "brute empiricism" alone, that is, by merely piling up more descriptive and more experimental data. What is elaborated and refined in theory is understanding, an ability to see relations more plainly, to conceptualize categories more accurately, and to create greater overall coherence in a subject, that is, to integrate its elements in a more logical, consistent, and intelligible fashion.

A problem arises when introducing theory into the study of personality and its disorders. Given an intuitive ability to "sense" the correctness of a psychological insight or speculation, theoretical efforts that impose structure or formalize these insights into a scientific system will be perceived not only as cumbersome and intrusive, but alien as well. This discomfiture and resistance does not arise in fields such as particle physics, where everyday observations are not readily available and where innovative insights are few and far between. In such subject domains, scientists are not only quite comfortable, but also turn readily to deductive theory as a means of helping them explicate and coordinate knowledge. It is paradoxical, but true and unfortunate, that personologists learn their subject quite well merely by observing the ordinary events of life. As a consequence of this ease, personologists appear to shy from and hesitate placing trust in the "obscure and complicating," yet often fertile and systematizing powers inherent in formal theory, especially theories that are new or that differ from those learned in their student days.

Adding to these hesitations is the fact that the formal structure of most personality theories is haphazard and un-systematic; concepts often are vague, and procedures by which empirical consequences may be derived are tenuous. Instead of presenting an orderly arrangement of concepts and proposi-tions by which hypotheses may be clearly derived, most theo-rists present a loosely formulated pastiche of opinions, analo-gies, and speculations. Brilliant as many of these speculations may be, they often leave the reader dazzled rather than illumi-nated. Ambiguous principles in structurally weak theories make it impossible to derive systematic and logical hypotheses; this results in conflicting derivations and circular reasoning. Many theories in both personality and psychopathology have generated brilliant deductions and insights, but few of these ideas can be attributed to their structure, the clarity of their central principles, the precision of their concepts, or their formal procedures for hypothesis derivation. It is here, of course, where the concepts and laws of adjacent sciences may come into play, providing models of structure and derivation, as well as substantive theories and data that may undergird and parallel the principles and observations of one's own field.

Despite the shortcomings in historic and contemporary theoretical schemas, systematizing principles and abstract concepts can "facilitate a deeper seeing, a more penetrating vision that goes beyond superficial appearances to the order underlying them" (Bowers, 1977). For example, pre-Darwinian taxonomists such as Linnaeus limited themselves to "apparent" similarities and differences among animals as a means of constructing their categories. Darwin was not "seduced" by appearances. Rather, he sought to understand the principles by which overt features came about. His classifications were based not only on descriptive qualities, but on explanatory ones.

CHAPTER TWO

THEORY I

Evolutionary Foundations of Physical and Biological Science

*T*hus, from the war of nature, from famine and death,
the most exalted object which we are capable of
conceiving, namely, the production of the higher animals,
directly follows . . . . While this planet has gone circling on
according to the fixed law of gravity, from so simple a
beginning endless forms most beautiful and most
wonderful have been, and are being evolved
(Darwin, 1859).

It is in both the spirit and substance of Darwin's "explanatory principles" that the reader should approach the proposals that follow. The principles employed are essentially the same as those which Darwin developed in seeking to explicate the origins of species. However, they are listed to derive—not the origins of species—but the structure and style of each of the personality disorders that are described in the *DSM-III-R* on the basis of clinical observation alone. Aspects of these formulations have been published in earlier books (Millon, 1969, 1981, 1986a), but they are anchored explicitly to evolutionary and ecological theory for the first time in this work. Identified in earlier writings as a biosocial learning model for personality and psychopathology, the theory has sought to generate the recognized categories of personality disorder through formal processes of deduction. A similar deductive process will be presented here.

To propose that fruitful ideas may be derived by applying evolutionary principles to the development and functions of personologic traits has a long, if yet unfulfilled, tradition. Spencer (1870) and Huxley (1870) offered suggestions of this nature shortly after Darwin's seminal *Origins* was published. The school of "functionalism," popular in psychology in the early part of this century, likewise drew its impetus from evolutionary concepts as it sought to articulate a basis for individual difference typologies (McDougall, 1908).

In more recent times, we have seen the emergence of sociobiology, a new "science" that explores the interface between human social functioning and evolutionary biology (Wilson, 1975, 1978). Contemporary formulations by psychologists have likewise proposed the potentials and analyzed the problems involved in cohering evolutionary notions, individual differences, and personality traits (A. Buss, 1987, D. Buss, 1984). The common goal among these proposals is not only the desire to apply analogous principles across diverse scientific realms, but also to reduce the enormous range of trait concepts and typologies that have proliferated through history. This goal might be achieved by exploring the power of evolutionary theory to simplify and order previously disparate personologic features. For example, all organisms seek to avoid injury, find nourishment, and reproduce their kind if they are to survive and maintain their populations. Each species displays commonalities in its adaptive or survival style. Within each species, however, there are differences in style and differences in the success with which its various members adapt to the diverse and changing environments they face. In these simplest of terms, personality would be conceived as representing the more-or-less distinctive style of adaptive functioning that an organism of a particular species exhibits as it relates to its typical range of environments. "Disorders" of personality, so formulated, would represent particular styles of maladaptive functioning that can be traced to deficiencies, imbalances, or conflicts in a species' capacity to relate to the environments it faces.

Before elaborating where these "disorders" arise within the human species, a few more words must be said concerning analogies between evolution and ecology, on the one hand, and personality, on the other.

During its life history an organism develops an assemblage of traits that contribute to its individual survival and reproductive success, the two essential components of "fitness" formulated by Darwin. Such assemblages, termed "complex adaptations" and "strategies" in the literature of evolutionary ecology, are close biological equivalents to what psychologists have conceptualized as personality styles and structures. In biology, explanations of a life history strategy of adaptations refer primarily to biogenic variations among constituent traits, their overall covariance structure, and the nature and ratio of favorable to unfavorable ecologic resources that have been available for purposes of extending longevity and optimizing reproduction. Such explanations are not appreciably different from those used to account for the development of personality styles or functions.

Bypassing the usual complications of analogies, a relevant and intriguing parallel may be drawn between the phylogenic evolution of a species' genetic composition and the ontogenic development of an individual organism's adaptive strategies (i.e., its "personality style"). At any point in time, a species will possess a limited set of genes that serve as trait potentials. Over succeeding generations the frequency distribution of these genes will likely change in their relative proportions depending on how well the traits they undergird contribute to the species' "fittedness" within its varying ecological habitats. In a similar fashion, individual organisms begin life with a limited subset of their species' genes and the trait potentials they subserve. Over time the *salience* of these trait potentials—not the proportion of the genes themselves—will become differentially prominent as the organism interacts with its environments. It "learns" from these experiences which of its traits "fit" best, that is, most optimally suited to its ecosystem. In phylogenesis, then, actual gene *frequer cies* change during the generation-to-generation adaptive pro_ess, whereas in ontogenesis it is the *salience* or prominence of gene-based traits that changes as adaptive learning takes place. Parallel evolutionary processes occur, one within the life of a species, the other within the life of an organism. What is seen in the individual organism is a shaping of latent potentials into adaptive and manifest styles of perceiving, feeling, thinking and acting; these distinctive ways of adaptation, engendered by the interaction of biologic endowment and social experience, comprise the elements of what is termed personality styles. It is a formative process in a single lifetime that parallels gene redistributions among species during their evolutionary history.

Two factors beyond the intrinsic genetic trait potentials of advanced social organisms have a special significance in affecting their survival and replicability. First, other members of the species play a critical part in providing postnatal nurturing and complex role models. Second, and no less relevant, is the high level of diversity and unpredictability of their ecological habitats. This requires numerous, multifaceted, and flexible response alternatives, either preprogrammed genetically or acquired subsequently through early learning. Humans are notable for unusual adaptive pliancy, acquiring a wide repertoire of "styles" or alternate modes of functioning for dealing both with predictable and novel environmental circumstances. Unfortunately, the malleability of early potentials for diverse learnings diminishes as maturation progresses. As a consequence, adaptive styles acquired in childhood, and usually suitable for comparable later environments, become increasingly immutable, resisting modification and relearning. Problems arise in new ecologic settings when these deeply ingrained behavior patterns persist, despite their lessened appropriateness; simply stated, what was learned and was once adaptive, may no longer "fit." Perhaps more important than environmental diversity, then, is the divergence between the circumstances of original learning and those of later life, a schism that has become more problematic as humans have progressed from stable and traditional to fluid and inconstant modern societies.

From the viewpoint of survival logic, it is both efficient and adaptive either to preprogram or to train the young of a species with traits that fit the ecologic habitats of their parents. This "wisdom" rests on the usually safe assumption that consistency, if not identicality will characterize the ecologic conditions of both parents and their offspring. Evolution is spurred when this continuity assumption fails to hold, that is, when formerly stable environments undergo significant change. Radical shifts of this character could result in the extinction of a species. It is more typical, however, for environments to be altered gradually, resulting in modest, yet inexorable redistributions of a species' gene frequencies. Genes which subserve competencies that prove suited to the new conditions become proportionately more common; ultimately, the features they engender come to typify either a new variant of, or a successor to the earlier species.

All animal species intervene in and modify their habitats in routine and repetitive ways. Contemporary humans are unique in evolutionary history, however, in that both the physical and social environment has been altered in precipitous and unpredictable ways; these interventions appear to have set in motion consequences not unlike the equilibrium "punctuations" theorized by modern paleontologists (Eldredge and Gould, 1972). This is best illustrated in the origins of our recent borderline personality "epidemic" (Millon, 1987a):

> Central to our recent culture have been the increased pace of social change and the growing pervasiveness of ambiguous and discordant customs to which children are expected to subscribe. Under the cumulative impact of rapid industrialization, immigration, urbanization, mobility, technology, and mass communication, there has been a steady erosion of traditional values and standards. Instead of a simple and coherent body of practices and beliefs, children find themselves confronted with constantly shifting styles and increasingly questioned norms whose durability is uncertain and precarious . . . . Few times in history have so many children faced the tasks of life without the aid of accepted and durable traditions. Not only does the strain of making choices among discordant standards and goals beset them at every turn, but these competing beliefs and divergent demands prevent them from developing either internal stability or external consistency (p. 363).

As recorded earlier, Murray has said that, "life is a continuous procession of explorations . . . learnings and relearnings" (1959). Yet, among species such as humans, early adaptive potentials and pliancies may fail to crystallize owing to the fluidities and inconsistencies of the environment, leading to the persistence of "immature and unstable styles" that fail to achieve coherence and effectiveness. Few can remain as flexible and functional as was Murray through his 100 years, less three.

Lest the reader assume that those seeking to wed the sciences of evolution and ecology find themselves fully welcome in their respective fraternities, there are those who assert that,

"despite pious hopes and intellectual convictions, [these two disciplines] have so far been without issue" (Lewontin, 1979). This judgment is now both dated and overly severe, but numerous conceptual and methodological impediments do face those who wish to bring these fields of biologic inquiry into fruitful synthesis—no less employing them to construe the styles and disorders of personality. Despite such concerns, recent developments bridging ecological and evolutionary theory are well underway, and hence do offer some justification for extending their principles to human styles of adaptation. To provide a conceptual background from these sciences, and to furnish a rough model concerning the styles of personality disorder, four domains or spheres in which evolutionary and ecological principles are demonstrated are labeled as *Existence, Adaptation, Replication,* and *Abstraction.* The first relates to the serendipitous transformation of random or less organized states into those possessing distinct structures of greater organization; the second refers to homeostatic processes employed to sustain survival in open ecosystems; the third pertains to reproductive styles that maximize the diversification and selection of ecologically effective attributes; and the fourth concerns the emergence of competencies that foster anticipatory planning and reasoned decision making.

Although the excursion presented here may merely be a psychological exercise, it should provide the open-minded reader with a contemporary perspective on evolutionary and ecological thought, one that encompasses all too briefly the origins of the universe, at one end, and the character of mind, at the other.

Existence: Serendipitous Transformations

Implicit in the concept of evolution is the notion of a forward direction. Difficulties arise, however, in trying to define pre-

cisely what forward direction means. Does it mean "progress," and by what gauges do we determine this progress? Is it moving from lower, or simpler, or less specialized to higher, or more complex, or more specialized forms? Is it an irreversible process, and are there no exceptions? Does it signify a sequence from less to more probable states, or from decreasing to increasing levels of organization? Unfortunately, positive replies to questions such as these usually replace ambiguous terms with others equally ill-defined, for example, exactly how and with reference to what attributes is "organizational level" to be measured? And even if evidence could be adduced that there has been a progression of increasing organization over time, that would merely provide a descriptive fact, not a principle or law of evolution, that is, one that follows as an inexorable consequence of the intrinsic properties of either matter or life.

A less troublesome and ultimately more satisfactory characterization of evolution is achieved when it is paired with the principles of ecology. So conceived, the "procession" of evolution represents no more than a series of serendipitous transformations in the structure of a phenomenon (e. g., elementary particle, chemical molecule, living organism) which appear to promote survival in both its current and future environments. Such processions usually stem from the consequences of either random fluctuations (e. g., mutations) or replicative reformations (e. g., recombinant mating) among an infinite number of possibilities—some simpler, others more complex, some more and others less organized, some increasingly specialized and others not. Evolution is defined, then, when these restructurings enable a natural entity (e. g., species) or its subsequent variants to survive within present and succeeding ecologic milieus. It is the continuity through time of these fluctuations and reformations that comprise the sequence we characterize as evolutionary progression.

The procession of evolution is not limited just to the evolution of life on earth, but extends to prelife, of matter, of the primordial elements of our local cosmos and, in all likelihood,

to the elusive properties of a more encompassing universe within which our cosmos is embedded as an incidental part. The demarcations conceptualized to differentiate states such as nonmatter and matter, or inorganic and organic, are nominal devices that record transitions in this ongoing procession of transformations, an unbroken sequence of re-formed elements that have existed from the very first.

One can speak of the emergence of our local cosmos from some larger universe, or of life from inanimate matter, but to trace the procession of evolution backward all the way would cause difficulty in identifying precise markers for each transition. As a definition, life would become progressively less clear as time reversed until its presence could no longer be discerned in the matter being studied. So, too, does it appear to theoretical physicists that to trace the evolution of our present cosmos back to its ostensive origins, its existence would be lost in the obscurity of an undifferentiated and unrecoverable past. The so-called "Big Bang" may in fact be merely an evolutionary transformation, one of an ongoing series of transitions in which the four dimensions that characterize our present universe emerged from a meta-universe of fluctuating entropic disorder, or from a mega-universe composed of many dimensions beyond those we apprehend.

The notion of open systems is of relatively recent origin (Bertalanffy, 1945; Lotka, 1924; Schrodinger, 1944), brought to bear initially to explain how the inevitable consequences of the Second Law of Thermodynamics appear to be circumvented in the biologic realm. By broadening the ecologic field so as to encompass events and properties beyond the local and immediate, it becomes possible to understand how living organisms on earth function and thrive, despite seeming to contradict this immutable physical law (e.g., solar radiation, continuously transmitting its ultimately exhaustible supply of energy, temporarily counters earth's inevitable thermodynamic entropy). The open-system concept has been borrowed freely and fruitfully to illuminate processes across a wide range of subjects,

from the work of Prigogine (1972) in articulating modes of self-organization in chemical kinetics, to contemporary psychotherapists who favor family or social system models.

Only in recent decades has the open-system concept been extended, albeit speculatively, to account for the evolution of cosmic events. These hypotheses suggest that the cosmos as known today represents but a four-dimensional "bubble" or set of "strings" stemming either from the random fluctuations of an open meta-universe characterized primarily by entropic chaos, or of transpositions from a larger set of dimensions that comprise the properties of an open mega-universe.

These formulations extend the boundaries of the Big Bang theory, which not only fails to account for many of the features of the cosmic firmament but limits expansion and transformations to elements within the confines of our local, closed space-time cosmos. By opening a "cocoon" to phenomena transcending immediate and proximal conditions, extending it to a meta- or to a mega-universe, cosmogony becomes but one phase of a series of evolutionary transformations, another transitional restructuring among infinite possibilities.

Predilections between the meta- versus mega-universe models favor a "nonspace-time" world composed of thermodynamic equilibrium, that is, a perfect entropic state of constant temperature and uniform disorder, from which periodic fluctuations of an entirely random character materialize states of order, most of which either collapse, are annihilated, or simply disappear, losing their transitory structure and decomposing back into the vast entropic chaos of nonspace-time equilibrium (nothingness?). In 1973, the first mathematization of this highly speculative proposal was presented by the theoretical physicist Edward Tryon; it has recently been developed further by the Russian theorists Alexander Vilenkin and Andrei Linde (Gribbin, 1986). They state that our cosmos is but a fluctuation of a vacuum that comprises an infinite meta-universe; the expansion that characterizes our local cosmos stems from a "big whoosh" that blew a tiny speck of a space-time fluctuation into its current enormous and expanding size.

Replacing the Big Bang with an open-system model, these formulations no longer need assume that all matter existing in our present-day cosmos was present within it at the moment of its expansion.

By materializing new matter from fluctuations in a larger and unstable field, that is, creating existence from nonexistence (perhaps "dark matter"), any embedded open system might not only expand, but form entities displaying "anti-entropic" structure, the future survival of which being determined by the character of parallel materializations and the fortuitous consequences of their interactions (i.e., their ecologic balance, symbiosis, and so on). Beyond fortuitous levels of reciprocal "fitness," some of these anti-entropic structures may possess properties that enable them to facilitate their own self-organization, that is, the forms into which they have been rendered randomly may not only "survive," but be able to amplify themselves and/or to extend their range, sometimes in replicated and sometimes in more comprehensive structures.

Recent mathematical research in both physics and chemistry has begun to elucidate processes that characterize how structures "evolve" from randomness. It is not only to complete this discussion of the essentially serendipitous nature of evolutionary processions that requires a few more words, but Murray (1959) himself was intrigued by patterns he observed in his own diverse studies years before it took on its current developments:

> The radical developments during the embryonic period led me to stress the concept of progressive disequilibrium, continuity through expansive, constructive change, as a supplement to that of homeostasis . . . . Less striking to the eye and less susceptible to precise measurement, are the seasons of transitional equilibrium on the psychological level, which occur most obviously in childhood but also later, during the early phases of some new enterprise, let us say, or when the creative imagination is steadily advancing. At such

times psychological processes are transformative, and when they terminate, the person is a different person, or his sphere of relationships is different, and there is a different equilibrium to be sustained.

To some readers I may appear to have digressed from the principal focus of this text in my excursion into cosmogony. However, a note or two more on seemingly tangential processes may not be entirely out of order; it is quite evident from the preceding quote by Murray that he did not hesitate to encompass sources seemingly removed from the task at hand, believing that they provide not only a perspective, but a means of seeing what we are grappling with more clearly. Nevertheless, a brief description of recent conceptions that relate to the very nature of existence and, more specifically, to that which differentiates order from disorder follows.

Whether one evaluates the character of cosmogenesis, the dynamics of open chemical systems, or repetitive patterns exhibited among weather movements, it appears that random fluctuations assume sequences that often become both self-sustaining and recurrent. In chemistry, the *theory of dissipative* (free energy) *structures* (Prigogine, 1972; 1976) proposes a principle called "order through fluctuation" that relates to self-organizational dynamics; these fluctuations proceed through sequences that not only maintain the integrity of the system, but are self-renewing. According to the theory, any open system may evolve when fluctuations exceed a critical threshold, setting in motion a qualitative shift in the nature of the system's structural form. Similar shifts within evolving systems are explained in pure mathematics by what has been termed *catastrophe theory* (Thom, 1972); here, sudden "switches" from one dynamic equilibrium state to another occur instantaneously with no intervening bridge. As models portraying how the dynamics of random fluctuation drive prior levels of equilibrium to reconstitute themselves into new structures, both catastrophe and dissipative theories prove fruitful in explicating self-evolving morphogenesis, that is, the emergence of new forms of existence from prior states.

Indirectly related to the preceding are recent mathematical studies into orderly and repetitive patterns that emerge when examining natural phenomena which appear random and unpredictable. Principles of "chaology" (Gleick, 1987) pertain both to states of disorder that lie beneath a facade of order, as well as to forms of organization that may be deeply hidden within seeming chaos. Random fluctuations and irregularities in ostensibly chaotic states may come to form not only complicated rhythms and patterns, but also demonstrate both recurrencies and replicated designs, such as seen in geometric "fractal" patterns (Mandelbrot, 1977); here, the same shapes emerge from fluctuations time and again, taking form sequentially on smaller and smaller scales.

Before closing this discussion on the emergence of newly evolved structures, there is a second and equally necessary step to survival, one that maintains "being" by protecting established forms of existence. Here the degrading effects of entropy are counteracted by a diversity of "safeguarding" mechanisms. Among inorganic substances, such as atoms and molecules, the elements comprising their nuclear structure are tightly bound, held together by the "strong force" that is exceptionally resistant to decomposition (hence the power necessary to "split" the atom). More complicated organic structures, such as plants and animals, also have mechanisms to counter entropic dissolution, that is, maintain the existence of their "life." Two intertwined strategies are required, one to achieve existence, the other to preserve it. The first aim is the *enhancement* of life, that is, creating or enriching ecologically survivable organisms; the second is oriented to the *preservation* of life, that is, avoiding events which might terminate it. Although I disagree with Freud's concept of a death instinct (Thanatos), I believe he was essentially correct in recognizing that a balanced, yet fundamental biological bipolarity exists in nature, a bipolarity that has its parallel in the physical world. As he wrote in one of his last works: "The analogy of our two basic instincts extends from the sphere of living things to the pair of opposing forces—attraction and repulsion—which rule the inorganic world" (Freud, 1940). Among humans, the former may be seen in life-*enhancing* acts which are "attracted" to what we experientially record as "pleasurable" events (positive reinforcers), the latter in life-*preserving* behaviors oriented to "repell" events experientially characterized as "painful" (negative reinforcers). More will be said of these fundamental, if not universal mechanisms of enriching existence and countering entropic disintegration in our next section.

Adaptation: Homeostatic Sustenance

To come into existence as an emergent particle, a local cosmos, or a living creature is but an initial phase, the serendipitous presence of a newly formed structure, the chance evolution of a phenomenon distinct from its surrounds. Though extant, such fortuitous transformations may exist only for a fleeting moment. Most emergent phenomena do not survive, that is, possess properties which enable them to retard entropic decomposition. To maintain their unique structure, differentiated from the larger ecosystem of which they are a part, to be sustained as a discrete entity among other phenomena that comprise their environmental field, requires good fortune and the presence of effective modes of adaptation. These modes of basic survival comprise the second essential component of evolution's procession; they will be discussed briefly in the following paragraphs.

As elaborated in the preceding section, *existence* is defined as a "to be" or "not to be" matter. At the organic level, the aims of existence were framed in terms of two polarities: those events which override entropy and thereby *enhance* life (i.e., what is experienced as pleasure) at one extreme and, at the other, those which circumvent entropy and thereby *preserve* life (i.e., what minimizes pain). The second evolutionary stage relates to what is termed the *modes of adaptation*; it is also framed as a two-part polarity. The first may best be characterized as the mode of *ecologic accommodation*, signifying inclinations to passively "fit in," to locate and remain securely anchored in a niche, subject to the vagaries and unpredictabilities of the environment, all acceded to with one crucial proviso: that the elements comprising the surrounds will furnish both the nourishment and the protection needed to sustain existence, i.e., survival. Though based on a somewhat simplistic bifurcation among adaptive strategies, this passive and accommodating mode is one of the two fundamental methods which living organisms have evolved as a means of survival. It represents the core process employed in the evolution of what has come to be designated the "plant kingdom," a stationary, rooted, yet essentially pliant and dependent survival mode. By contrast, the second of the two major modes of adaptation is seen in the lifestyle of the "animal kingdom." Here we observe a primary inclination toward *ecologic modification*, a tendency to change or rearrange the elements comprising the larger milieu, to intrude on otherwise quiescent settings, a versatility in shifting from one niche to another as unpredictability arises, a mobile and interventional mode that actively stirs, maneuvers, yields and, at the human level, substantially transforms the environment to meet its own survival aims.

Of interest here is that it was Aristotle who first drew the basic biological distinction between organisms capable of absorbing nutrients only in a fixed location and those able to move about in their search for nourishment. Referred to as autotrophs, or self-feeders, plants are sessile, that is, immobile and permanently fixed in an ecologic niche. In such settings, they are the recipients, with little or no action on their part, of solar energy and inorganic nutrients (water, gases, minerals) necessary to grow and sustain their cellular structures. Animals, by contrast, are termed heterotrophs, or other-feeders. Unable to survive on the inorganic nutrients of the soil alone, nor capable of drawing "free energy" from solar radiation, they must search and consume preformed organic matter to sustain themselves, such as found in the carbohydrates, proteins and fats of other living creatures. Both modes—passive and active—have proven impressively capable of both nourishing and preserving life.

Whether the polarity we have sketched is phrased in terms of accommodating versus modifying, passive versus active, or plant versus animal, it represents, at the most basic level, the two fundamental modes which organisms have evolved to sustain their existence. This second aspect of evolution differs from the first stage, that concerned with what may be called existential "becoming," in that it characterizes modes of "being," that is, how what has become endures.

The origins of these modes are uncertain. Given their ancestry and the varied environments within which organismic evolution has taken its diverse forms, most morphologic structures serve multiple functions; versatility characterizes the biologic substrates of complex organisms. As new structural configurations evolve in response to ecologic circumstance, gene mutation, and chromosomal recombination, they intermesh and conform to the extant arrangement of an organism's morphologic constitution. These new configurations generate countless unanticipated potentials, competencies and capabilities that may prove richer and more diverse in their adaptive value than those which activated them initially. Hence, it is not only ecologic circumstance that precipitates newly emergent adaptations, but equally and often more facilitative are these coincidentally forged capacities and versatilities.

Much can be said for the survival value of fitting a specific niche well, but no less important are flexibilities for adapting to diverse and unpredictable environments. It is here again where a distinction, though not a hard and fast one, may be drawn between the accommodating (plant) and the modifying (animal) mode of adaptation, the former more rigidly fixed and constrained by ecologic conditions, the latter more broad-ranging and more facile in its scope of maneuverability. To proceed in evolved complexity to the human species one cannot help but recognize the almost endless variety of adaptive possibilities that may (and do) arise as secondary derivatives of a large brain possessing an open network of potential interconnections that permit the functions of self-reflection, reasoning, and abstraction. But this takes us ahead of the current subject.

It should be noted that optimal functioning calls for a flexible balance that incorporates the range between both polar extremes. In the first evolutionary stage, that relating to "existence," competencies permitting both the enhancement of life (pleasure) and life-preservation (pain avoidance) are likely to be more successful in achieving survival than actions limited to one or the other alone. Similarly, regarding "adaptation," modes of functioning that employ both ecologic accommodation and ecologic modification are likely to be more successful than either by itself.

Despite the advantages of flexibility, it appears that the two advanced forms of life on earth—plants and animals—give precedence to one mode rather than the other. Whichever is primary, its essential function, as Schrodinger (1944) has put it, is to sustain an organism at a stable and organized level by "sucking orderliness" from its environment, that is, receiving more energy than it expends to harvest it. The nutrients drawn into its system must be richer in energy than that which it returns to inanimate nature, compensating along the way for the costs of metabolism.

Favorable exchanges of energy with host environments are evident also in both growth and reproduction. In these functions, organisms not only resist entropy, but achieve a measurable, if temporary, decrease in it. Organisms may be sustained in ways that differ from the fully mature mode as they progress through development, for example, embryonic humans are rooted, whereas adults are mobile. In their mature stage organisms possess the requisite competencies to maintain entropic stability. When these competencies can no longer sustain homeostasis, the organism succumbs inexorably to death and decomposition. This fate does not signify finality, however. Prior to its demise, all species create duplicates which circumvent their extinction, engaging in acts that enable them to transcend the entropic dissolution of their members' individual existences.

Replication: Selective Diversification

If an organism merely duplicates itself prior to death, then its replica is "doomed" to repeat the same fate it suffered. However, if new potentials for extending existence can be fashioned by chance or routine events, then the possibility of achieving a different and conceivably superior outcome may be increased. It is the co-occurrence of random and recombinant processes which leads to the prolongation of a species' existence; it is also the third hallmark of evolution's procession.

Life arose when molecular aggregates formed a complex system capable of reproducing itself. Some three billion years later, over a million animal species and a half-million species of plants inhabited the earth, ranging in size from submicroscopic viruses to 90-foot-long whales and 400-foot-tall trees. Diverse in form and function, they burrowed underground, swam the seas, soared in the air, raced across the land, or remained rooted, immobile in the soil. Why and how did the primeval assemblage unfold into so diverse a range of living and reproducing systems?

The answer is a simple one, though it would be foolhardy, even if space and knowledge permitted, to attempt to explicate the many particulars this question can elicit. At its most basic and universal level, the manifold varieties of organisms living today have evolved, as Mayr (1964) has phrased it, to cope with the challenge of continuously changing and immensely diversified environments, the resources of which are not inexhaustible.

The basic means by which organisms have evolved to cope with environmental change and diversity are well-known. Inorganic structures survive for extended periods of time by virtue of the extraordinary strength of their bonding. This contrasts with the very earliest forerunners of organic life. Until they could replicate themselves, their distinctive assemblages existed precariously, subject to events that could put a swift end to the discrete and unique qualities that characterized their composition, leaving them essentially as transient and ephemeral phenomena. Once replicative procedures were perfected, the chemical machinery for copying organismic life, the DNA double helix, became so precise that it could produce perfect clones, *if* nothing interfered with its structure or its mechanisms of execution. But the patterning and processes of complex molecular change are not immune to accident. High temperatures and radiation dislodge and rearrange atomic structures, producing what has been termed mutations, alterations in the controlling and directing DNA configuration that undergirds the replication of organismic morphology. No facet of any microorganism, plant, or animal has escaped the chance effects of mutation, be it in their size, strength, color, composition, metabolism, or longevity.

Despite the deleterious impact of most mutations, it is the genetic variations they give rise to which have served as the primary means by which simple organisms acquire traits capable of adapting to diverse and changing environments. With new generations reproduced every several minutes, and with enormous populations of billions on billions of individuals in the reproductive chain, the rare emergence of beneficent mutations occur with sufficient frequency to establish new potentials capable of meeting a host of ecologic challenges.

But isomorphic replication, aided by an occasional beneficent mutation, is a most inefficient, if not hazardous means of surmounting ecologic crises faced by complex and slowly reproducing organisms. Advantageous mutations do not appear in sufficient numbers and with sufficient dependability to generate the novel capabilities required to adapt to frequent or marked shifts in the ecosystem. How then did the more intricate and intermittently reproducing organisms evolve the means to resolve the diverse hazards of unpredictable environments?

The answer that evolved in response to this daunting task was the emergence of a recombinant mechanism, one in which a pair of organisms exchanged their genetic resources, that is, they developed what we term sexual mating. Here, the potentials and traits each partner possesses are sorted into new configurations that differ in their compositions from those of their origins, generating thereby new variants and capabilities, of which some may prove more adaptive (and others less or adaptively irrelevant) in changing environments than their antecedents. Great advantages do accrue by the occasional favorable combinations that occur through this random shuffling of genes. The continuous diversification from generation to generation through ever-new adaptive configurations are tested repeatedly by the challenges and demands of everchanging environments. With only rare individuals genetically identical (e.g., the uncommon twin), a selective process unfolds in which the ecologically most competent combinations survive and replicate further, encouraging thereby a continuous flow of new potentials for adaptation.

Sexual methods of recombinant replication, with their consequential benefits of selective diversification, require the partnership of two "parents," each contributing its genetic resources in a distinctive and species' characteristic manner. Similarly, the attention and care given the offspring of a species' matings is also distinctive. Worthy of special note is the difference between the mating parents in the degree to which they protect and nourish their joint offspring. Although the investment of energy devoted to upbringing is balanced and complementary, rarely is it identical or even comparable in either devotion or determination. This disparity in reproductive "investment" strategies, especially evident among animal species (insects, reptiles, birds, mammals), underlies the evolution of the male and female genders, the foundation for the third cardinal polarity we propose to account for evolution's procession.

Somewhat less profound than that of the first polarity, which represents the line separating the enhancement of order (existence-life) from the prevention of disorder (nonexistence-death), or that of the second polarity, differentiating the adaptive modes of accommodation (passive-plant) from those of modification (active-animal), the third polarity, based on distinctions in replication strategies, is no less fundamental in that it contrasts the maximization of reproductive propagation (self-male) from that of the maximization of reproductive nurturance (other-female).

Evolutionary biologists (Cole, 1954; Trivers, 1971; Wilson, 1975) have recorded marked differences among species in both the cycle and pattern of their reproductive behaviors. Of special interest is the extreme diversity among *and* within species in the number of offspring spawned and the consequent nurturing and protective investment the parents make in the survival of their progeny. Designated the *r*-strategy and *K*-strategy in population biology, the former represents a pattern of propagating a vast number of offspring, but exhibiting minimal attention to their survival, the latter typified by the production of few progeny, followed by considerable effort to assure their survival. Exemplifying the *r*-strategy are oysters, who generate some 500 million eggs annually; the *K*-strategy is found among the great apes who produce a single offspring every five to six years.

Not only do species differ in where they fall on the *r*- to *K*-strategy continuum, but within most animal species an important distinction may be drawn between male and female genders. It is this latter differentiation that undergirds what will be termed the *self* versus *other*-oriented polarity, implications of which will be briefly elaborated.

Despite the undeniable role of social tradition, most subhuman mammalian families are typified by a single, dominant male with multiple female partners; further, that three-fourths of all human societies not only permit multiple wives, but embody the practice of polygyny through informal or religious law. Polyandry, in contrast, is present in only about one percent of all human societies, as well as being quite infrequent in lower animals. What biologic processes undergird or govern these customs?

Human females typically produce about 400 eggs in a lifetime, of which no more than 20 to 25 can mature into healthy infants. The energy investment expended in gestation, nurturing, and caring for each child, both before and during the years following birth are extraordinary. Not only is the female required to devote much of her energies to bring the fetus to full term, but during this period she cannot be fertilized again; in contrast, the male is free to mate with numerous females. And should her child fail to survive, the waste in physical and emotional exertion is not only enormous, but amounts to a substantial portion of the mother's lifetime reproductive potential. There appears to be good reason, therefore, to expect a protective and caring inclination on the part of the female. This is evident in her sensitivity to cues of distress and a willingness to persist in attending to the needs and nurturing of her offspring.

Although the male discharges tens of millions of sperm on mating, this is but a small investment, given the ease and frequency with which he can repeat the act. On fertilization, his physical and emotional commitment can end with minimal consequences. Although the protective and food-gathering efforts of the male may be lost by an early abandonment of a mother and an offspring or two, much more may be gained by investing energies in pursuits that achieve the wide reproductive spread of his genes. Relative to the female of the species, whose best strategy appears to be the care and comfort of child and kin, that is, the K-strategy, the male is likely to be reproductively more prolific by maximizing self-propagation, that is, adopting the r-strategy. To focus primarily on self-replication may diminish the survival probabilities of a few of a male's progeny, but this occasional reproductive loss may be well compensated for by mating with multiple females, and thereby producing multiple offspring.

The consequences of the r-strategy are a broad range of what may be seen as self- as opposed to other-oriented behaviors, such as acting in an egotistic, insensitive, inconsiderate, uncaring, and noncommunicative manner. In contrast, females are more disposed to be other-oriented, affiliative, intimate, empathic, protective, and solicitous (Gilligan, 1982; Rushton, 1985; Wilson, 1978).

Lest there be misunderstanding, no sharp line separates the genders; rather, these inclinations lie on a continuum with "soft" group discriminations and substantial overlapping. Our intent is not to draw attention to gender differences per se, but rather to identify the existence of a deep, biologically grounded spectrum of dispositions in which the enhancement or propagation of *self* represents one polar extreme (the r-strategy), and the enhancement or nurturance of *others* represents the second (the K-strategy).

The three polarities we have outlined in this and the preceding sections are broad abstractions drawn from conceptions in physics and biology that may appear distally related to matters of psychological significance. It is my belief, however, that they may serve as a foundation on which we may base a deeper and perhaps clearer understanding of personality processes. Whether or not they prove useful in this regard, they reflect the origins of three of the most fundamental distinctions that have evolved in the history of earth: life versus death, plant versus animal, male versus female.

It may be noted in passing that the evolution from the first to third polarity corresponds also to important sequential progressions, only two of which will be touched on briefly. Phylogenically, for example, humans may be seen as having evolved from the genesis of *life*, to the active or *animal* mode of sustenance, and then to the division of *male* and *female* gender strategies. Ontogenically, the developmental sequence termed neuropsychological stages (Millon, 1969, 1981) advances from an initial and largely inborn "sensory-attachment" phase, oriented to discriminating *pleasure* from *pain* signals, to a "sensorimotor-autonomy" phase which enables the transition from a *passive accommodation* to a postnatal *active modification* of the environment, to the third or "intracortical-initiative" phase, in which the distinction between *self-propagating* and *other-nurturing* reproductive strategies take firm root.

Abstraction: Reflective Mind

The diverse cognitive features and adaptive competencies of intelligence will not be included as central elements in our personologic derivations. Nonetheless, they do comprise, in my judgment, what may be viewed to be the fourth and most recent phase of evolution. The reflective capacity to transcend the immediate and concrete, to interrelate and synthesize diversity, to represent events and processes symbolically, to weigh, reason and anticipate, each signifies a quantum leap in evolution's potential for change and adaptation. Emancipated from the real and present, unanticipated possibilities and novel constructions may routinely be created. The capacity to sort and to recompose, to coordinate and to arrange the symbolic representations of experience into new configurations is, in certain ways, analogous to the random processes of recombinant replication, but they are more focused and intentional. To extend this rhetorical liberty, replication is the recombinant mechanism underlying the adaptive progression of phylogeny, whereas abstraction is the recombinant mechanism underlying the adaptive progression of ontogeny. The powers of replication are limited, constrained by the finite potentials inherent in parental genes. In contrast, experiences, abstracted and recombined, are infinite. Over one lifetime, innumerable events of a random, logical, or irrational character transpire, construed and reformulated time and again, some of which proving more, and others less adaptive than their originating circumstances may have called forth. Whereas the actions of most subhuman species derive from successfully evolved genetic programs, activating behaviors of a relatively fixed nature suitable for a modest range of environmental settings, the capabilities of both implicit and intentional abstraction that characterize humans give rise to adaptive competencies that are suited to radically divergent ecologic circumstances, circumstances which themselves may be the result of far-reaching acts of symbolic and technologic creativity.

Although what underlies our self versus other-oriented attributes stems from differential replication strategies, the conscious state of "knowing" self, as distinct from others, is a product of the power of abstraction, the most recent phase of evolution's procession. The reflective process of turning inward and recognizing self as an object, no less to know oneself and, further, to know that one knows, is a uniqueness found only among humans. Doubling back on oneself, so to speak, creates a new level of "reality," consciousness that imbues "self" and "others" with properties far richer and more subtle than those which derive from strategies of reproductive propagation and nurturance alone.

The abstracting mind may mirror outer realities, but reconstructs them in the process, reflectively transforming them into subjective modes of phenomenologic reality, making external events into a plastic mold subject to creative designs. Not only are images of self and others emancipated from direct sensory realities, becoming entities possessing a life of their own, but contemporaneous time may also lose its immediacy and impact. The abstracting mind brings the past effectively into the present, and its power of anticipation brings the future into the present, as well. With past and future embedded in the here and now, humans can encompass, at once, not only the totality of our cosmos, but its origins and nature, its evolution, and how they have come to pass. Most impressive of all are the many visions humans have of life's indeterminate future, where no reality as yet exists.

CHAPTER THREE

THEORY II

Concordance of Evolutionary Polarities and Psychological Science

One evening last week when I was hard at work, tormented with just that amount of pain that seems to be the best state to make my brain function, the barriers were suddenly lifted, the veil was drawn aside, and I had a clear vision from the details of the neuroses to the conditions that make consciousness possible. Everything seemed to connect up, the whole worked well together, and one had the impression that the thing was now really a machine and would soon go by itself. . . . All that was perfectly clear, and still is (Freud, 1895).

Those acquainted with musical compositions will quickly recognize the evolving structure of these chapters. The "exposition" of key themes in the sonata form are presented in the opening "movement," stated in simple melodic lines, then developed through variations, contrasts, interweaving, and finally recapitulated in a later movement. The chain of reasoning being followed progresses in a similar fashion. Major themes have been stated; they will be rephrased, built on, unfolded, and recombined, taking forms apparently distinct from their foundations, yet ultimately brought full circle to points of origin. In simpler terms, the planned progression might be viewed as akin to waves at high tide, each built on those which preceded it, moving forward in incremental fashion, only to return in time to an earlier level.

The brief excursion into motifs derived within the realms of physical science lead to ideas conceived within the purview of biological science; in this chapter, the themes will connect to topics encompassed within psychological science; finally, in the next chapter we will seek to fashion our subject to fit the domain of personologic science. At root, each science shares common themes, although their forms and mechanisms differ appreciably. Explications of the structures and functions of each science will uncover patterns of organization and process that have evolved to counter entropic decomposition or to replicate extant structures, be it with mechanisms that serve to bond inorganic matter, or exhibit behaviors which aggrandize personal territory, or express themselves in reproductive mating.

The major polarities articulated earlier, cast here for the first time in evolutionary terms, have forerunners in psychological theory that may be traced as far back as the early 1900s. A number of pre-World War I theorists proposed a set of three polarities that were used time and again as the raw materials for constructing psychological processes. For example, Freud wrote in 1915 (1915/1925) what many consider to be among his most seminal papers, those on metapsychology and, in particular, the section entitled "Instincts and Their Vicissitudes." Speculations that foreshadowed several concepts developed more fully later, both by himself and others, were presented in preliminary form in these papers. Particularly notable is a framework that Freud advanced as central to understanding the mind; unfortunately, his basic scaffolding of three polarities was never developed by him as a system for conceptualizing personality structures and functions. It was framed as follows:

> . . . Our mental life as a whole is governed by three polarities, namely, the following antitheses:
>
> Subject (ego)-Object (external world)
>
> Pleasure-Pain
>
> Active-Passive
>
> The three polarities within the mind are connected with one another in various highly significant ways (1915, pp. 76–77).
>
> We may sum up by saying that the essential feature in the vicissitudes undergone by instincts is their subjection to the influences of the three great polarities that govern mental life. Of these three polarities we might describe that of activity-passivity as the biological, that of the ego-external world as the real, and finally that of pleasure-pain as the economic, respectively (1915, p. 83).

Aspects of Freud's three polarities were "discovered" and employed by theorists earlier than he—in France, Germany, Russia, and other European nations, as well as in the United States. Variations of the three dimensions of active-passive, subject-object, and pleasure-pain were identified by Heymans and Wiersma in Holland, McDougall in the United States, Meumann in Germany, Kollarits in Hungary, as well as others.

Despite the central role Freud assigned these polarities, he failed to capitalize on them as a basis for formulating personality types. Preoccupied with discovering the symptom derivatives of instincts as they unfold during psychosexual development, Freud showed little interest at the time in constructing a typology of character structures. Although he failed to pursue their potentials, the ingredients he formulated for his tripartite polarity schema were drawn on by his disciples for many decades to come, seen prominently in the recent growth of "ego psychology," "self-psychology," and "object relations" theory.

Forgotten as a metapsychological speculation by most, the scaffolding comprising these polarities was fashioned anew by this author in the mid-1960s (Millon, 1969). Unacquainted with Freud's proposals at the time, and employing a biosocial-learning model, the author constructed a framework similar to Freud's "great polarities that govern all of mental life." Phrased in the terminology of learning concepts, the biosocial model comprised three polar dimensions: (reinforcement nature): *positive-negative*; (reinforcement source): *self-other*; and (instrumental behavior): *active-passive*. As stated at the time (Millon, 1969):

> By framing our thinking in terms of *what* reinforcements the individual is seeking, *where* he is looking to find them and *how* he performs we may see more simply and more clearly the essential strategies which guide his coping behaviors.
>
> These reinforcements [relate to] whether he seeks primarily to achieve positive reinforcements (pleasure) or to avoid negative reinforcements (pain) . . . .
>
> Some patients turn to others as their source of reinforcement, whereas some turn primarily to themselves.

The distinction (is) between *others* and *self* as the primary reinforcement source.

On what basis can a useful distinction be made among instrumental behaviors? A review of the literature suggests that the behavioral dimension of activity-passivity may prove useful . . . . Active patients (are) busily intent on controlling the circumstances of their environment . . . . Passive patients . . . wait for the circumstances of their environment to take their course . . . reacting to them only after they occur (pp. 193–195).

Where do we find parallels within the discipline of psychology that correspond to the broad evolutionary polarities sketched in earlier sections?

In addition to the forerunners noted previously, there is a growing group of contemporary scholars whose work has begun to illuminate these polar dimensions, albeit indirectly and partially. For example, a tripartite model has been formulated over the last 30-year period by the distinguished British psychologist, Hans Eysenck (1957, 1967). A parallel, but more modern conception anchored to biological foundations has likewise been developed by Eysenck's erstwhile student Jeffrey Gray (1964, 1973). A three-part model of temperament, grounded in behavioral and evolutionary theory, and matching in most regards the three-part polarity model, has been formulated by the highly resourceful American psychologist, Arnold Buss and his associates (Buss and Plomin, 1975, 1984). Circumplex formats based on factor analytic studies of mood and arousal that align well with the author's schema have been published by Russell (1980) and Tellegen (1985). Deriving inspiration from a sophisticated analysis of neuroanatomical substrates, Cloninger (1986, 1987) has deduced a threefold schema that is coextensive with the model's three polarities. Oriented less to biological foundations, recent advances in both interpersonal and psychoanalytic theory likewise exhibit strong parallels to one or more of the three polar dimensions.

Before describing these and comparable formulations in the psychological literature, a few words should be said about the metaphorical and multireferential character of this field's conceptual language.

As we know, each discipline and subdiscipline construes its subject in the context of its unique history and traditions, focusing only on specific and narrow aspects of an intrinsically indivisible world, developing thereby a language particular to these traditions and areas of focus (Millon, 1967, 1969). As a consequence, similar, if not identical phenomena are conceived differently and given disparate labels. "Pain" or "anxiety" illustrate such multireferential and metaphorical concepts. Each of these terms may be defined or operationally anchored to a variety of empirical events, such as biochemical pathways, overt behavior, subjective reports, cognitive schemata, unconscious processes, as well as reifications, mixtures of all, and more. Complicating matters further, each construct's empirical referents may be employed to illustrate a wide and assorted range of concepts, e.g., facial expressions may serve to generate constructs that exemplify emotions, behaviors, attitudes, unconscious motives, and the like.

A further aside of a quasi-philosophical nature concerning "causal explanations" may also be useful as a preamble to the following discussion. It relates to a distinction between *proximal* and *distal* interpretations of a process or phenomenon, each of which may be "correct," depending on the timeframe and class of data to which questions of a scientific nature may be addressed (Millon, 1967). Thus, a proximal analysis of "pain" as an experience would likely center attention on properties and mechanisms of immediate or ontogenic causation, such as bodily areas subjected to direct organic damage, activated hormonal or CNS processes, conditioned learnings, cognitive attributions, locus of control, temperamental sensitivities, personality coping styles, and so on. Distal explanations would be inclined to search out the meaning or ultimate purpose served by proximal mechanisms, such as their existential significance, their adaptive role, their emergence through phylogenic history, their place and diverse expression in the evolution of organisms. Not only is pain multireferential (e.g., cognitive, emotional, behavioral), but both proximal and distal explanations serve useful and legitimate, if different, scientific purposes, as well as prove frequently to be complementary and reciprocally supportive.

With the preceding apologia in mind, the reader should approach the complex considerations which relate evolutionary polarities to their psychological parallels with both a sophisticated and tolerant outlook.

The Aims of Existence

Life Enhancement and Life Preservation: Pleasure-Pain Polarity

As described previously, existence reflects a "to be" or "not to be" issue. In the inorganic world "to be" is essentially a matter of possessing qualities which distinguish a phenomenon from its surrounding field, that is, not being in a state of entropy. Among organic beings, "to be" is a matter of possessing the properties of life, as well as being located in ecosystems that facilitate the preservation and enhancement of that life. In the phenomenological or experiential world of sentient organisms, events that extend life and preserve it correspond largely to metaphorical terms such as "pleasure" and "pain," that is, eliciting positive sensations and emotions, on the one hand, and eschewing negative sensations and emotions, on the other.

The pleasure-pain distinction recognizes that sensations, motivations, feelings, emotions, moods, and affects can ultimately be placed on two contrasting dimensions, each possessing separate quantitative extremes (i.e., bipolarities)—events such as attractive, gratifying, rewarding, or positively reinforcing may be experienced as weak or strong, as can those which are aversive, distressful, sad or negatively reinforcing also be experienced as weak or strong. Not only may each dimension operate independently of the other, but efforts to identify specific events or experiences that fit each pole of the pleasure-pain bipolarity are likely to distract from the essential distinction. Thus, the particular actions or objects that people find pleasurable (e.g., sex, sports, art, or money) are legion, and for every patient who experiences a certain event as rewarding, one can find another who experiences that same event as distasteful or painful; for example, some patients who are driven to seek attention are sexually promiscuous, whereas others are repelled by sexuality in any form. In short, categorizations based on the specific properties of what may be subsumed under the broad constructs of pain or pleasure will prove not only futile and cumbersome, but misguiding as well.

Since the higher centers of our brain are guided by reflective and rational calculation, decisions that must be taken quickly or automatically are best guided by readily activated sensations, such as those of pleasure and pain, signals mediated by primitive centers of the brain formed early in evolutionary history. Hypotheses derived from evolutionary theory require that these signals, be they "painful" anticipatory anxiety or "pleasurably" exhilarating sex are aroused when events have either gone awry or are likely to enhance personal or reproductive survival.

Darwin was the first to provide a scientifically plausible analysis of how species evolved phylogenically to perform increasingly adaptive behaviors, but it was his contemporary, Herbert Spencer, who gave the first scientifically plausible explanation of how the behaviors of organisms were differentially strengthened ontogenically to perform increasingly adaptive behaviors. Although he was anticipated by Spinoza (1677/ 1986), this brief review of psychological constructs that parallel the pleasure-pain bipolarity begins with Herbert Spencer, who not only wrote directly and extensively of the role of "pleasures and pains" in his treatise, *The Principles of Psychology* (1870), but set forth what Thorndike later termed the *Law of Effect* (1905), a principle from which much research and discussion on the nature of learning was based for the next half-century, and the source from which Skinner formulated his productive concepts of positive and negative reinforcers.

While aware of the many philosophical and meta-psychological issues associated with the "nature" of pain and pleasure as constructs, it is neither our intent nor our task, however, to inquire into them here. Rather, we will limit ourselves to demonstrating that they recur as a polar dimension time and again in such diverse psychological domains as *learned behaviors, unconscious processes, emotion and motivation,* as well as their *biological substrates.*

Positive and Negative Reinforcers of Learning

Among Spencer's major contributions, often overlooked among those who trace their conceptions of reinforcement learning to twentieth-century thinkers, is that organisms repeat actions that bring pleasure, and discontinue those which bring pain. Quoting Spencer (1870):

> Pains are the correlatives of actions injurious to the organism, while pleasures are the correlatives of actions conducive to its welfare.

> Those races of beings only can have survived in which, on the average, agreeable or desired feelings went along with activities conducive to the maintenance of life, while disagreeable and habitually avoided feelings went along with activities directly or indirectly destructive of life.

> Every animal habitually persists in each act which gives pleasure, so long as it does so, and desists from each act

which gives pain . . . . It is manifest that in proportion as this guidance approaches completeness, the life will be long; and that the life will be short in proportion as it falls short of completeness.

We accept the inevitable corollary from the general doctrine of Evolution, that pleasures are the incentives to life-supporting acts and pains the deterrents from life-destroying acts. (pp. 279–284).

Judging the preceding to be self-evident, Spencer sought to furnish a "scientific" underpinning to his conceptions of pain and pleasure. As with his twentieth-century successors, Spencer offered plausible, if highly conjectural neurological speculations to account for his observations. Although different in their particulars, Spencer foreshadowed the ideas of a similar nature by Pavlov and Freud in arguing that both the experience of pleasure and its reinforcing properties could be traced to increments in nervous system excitation; conversely, feelings of pain and their consequences were connected to decrements or inhibitions in this activity.

The Law of Effect was so named in Thorndike's first text, *The Elements of Psychology* (1905); he offered a physiologic explanation for its action in a paper three years later (1908), stating that the nervous system is arranged so as to lead to the strengthening of connections that were active just prior to a satisfying event, and to the weakening of those connections that were active just prior to an annoying event. As for the Law of Effect itself, Thorndike wrote (1932):

Of several responses made to the same situation, those which are accompanied or closely followed by satisfaction to the animal will, other things being equal, be more firmly connected with the situation, so that, when it recurs, they will be more likely to recur; those which are accompanied or closely followed by discomfort to the animal will, other things being equal, have their connections with that situation weakened, so that, when it recurs, they will be less likely to occur. The greater the satisfaction or discomfort, the greater the strengthening or weakening of the bond (p. 234).

Thorndike modified aspects of his learning formulations during his long career, but the key role of satisfaction (pleasure) and discomfort (pain) remained central to his thesis. Although "noneffect" theorists gained considerable recognition during the midpart of this century, few dismissed the impact that pleasure or pain might bring to the learning process; thus, for Tolman, the first major cognitive-learning theorist (1932), rewards and punishments were conceived as "emphasizers," rather than strengtheners or weakeners of a learned connection.

Turning to the major learning "theorist" of the midmind of this century, B. F. Skinner (1938, 1953), primacy is given again to the pleasure-pain bipolarity, termed in his atheoretical and antisubjective phrasing as positive reinforcers and negative reinforcers. Eschewing both internal and judgmental processes, which lead to words such as pleasant or unpleasant, Skinner's use of the consequences of pleasure and pain for his conception of learning is evident in the following quote (1953):

Events which are found to be reinforcing are of two sorts. Some reinforcements consist of presenting stimuli, of adding something—for example, food, water, or sexual contact—to the situation. These we call *positive* reinforcers. Others consist of removing something—for example, a loud noise, a very bright light, extreme cold or heat, or electric shock—from the situation. These we call *negative* reinforcers. In both cases the effect of reinforcement is the same—the probability of response is increased (p. 73).

Instinctual Aims of the Id

As noted in previous pages, Freud framed a tripartite polarity schema of contrasting orientations which together "govern all of mental life"; included among them was the bipolar antithesis of pleasure-pain (Freud, 1915/1925). Despite Freud's efforts to explicate numerous expressions of and significant roles for the pleasure principle, the primary aim of the "id," clinical professions primarily attend to the varied manifestations of "pain," such as anxiety and depression. It is understandable why clinical theorists preoccupy themselves with pathologic syndromes, but it seems unfortunate that they have overlooked Freud's view that the pleasure-oriented drives of the id not only express the "life instincts" in both sexual and self-preservation forms, but are the source of self and object cathexes, manifest themselves in the maturation of a crucial stage-specific developmental sequence, as well as in its diverse characterologic consequences.

Referring to his colleagues' seeming disinterest in the psychologic significance of "pleasure," Henry Murray commented (1952):

> One of the strangest, least interpretable symptoms of our time is the neglect by psychologists of the problem of happiness . . . . Although the crucial role of dissatisfaction and of satisfaction is implicit in much that is said about motivation, activity, and reinforcement, psychologists are generally disposed to shun these terms . . . .
>
> Be that as it may, satisfaction is an affective state which is likely to manifest itself objectively as well as subjectively. It is no more difficult to diagnose than anxiety or anger, and, in my opinion, should be thoroughly investigated (pp. 455–456).

Although Freud equated instinctual gratification (pleasure) with tension discharge, a view leading to his initial extrapolation to the problematic death instinct, more recent analytic formulations conceive pleasure either as a signal of "safety or hope," or a feeling that "something has been added," a life-enhancing mastery, a progressing relationship, a substantive or even illusory gain for the ego (Szasz, 1975). However interpreted, "hedonic" signals stand as one of the two pillars that undergird the pleasure-pain bipolarity, one of the three antitheses that "govern mental life."

As for the concept of pain, it is viewed in contemporary analytic circles as a generic concept that subsumes several principal clinical entities, such as anxiety and depression, as well as their innumerable forms of expression. Briefly, anxiety continues to be viewed much as Freud originally conceived it, a signal that "danger lies ahead" (Fenichel, 1945), more specifically that one stands to lose either self, part of self, or a significant or needed object. Often mixed with anxiety as a composite experience of pain, depression is less a signal than a consequence, one felt when a loss has already or is in the process of occurring. Our intent here is only to illustrate the central importance given pain—and pleasure—in different and diverse spheres of psychological inquiry, not to elaborate the weighty clinical entities of depression and anxiety.

Pleasant and Unpleasant Valences of Emotion

This section addresses subject realms within which the concepts of pain and pleasure fit most directly—emotion, mood, motivation, and temperament. The two previously discussed domains of learning and of unconscious processes focused on topics which gave emotions and motivations an important, but secondary role; yet, as illustrated briefly, pain and pleasure proved to be centrally involved in their respective formulations. Does the bipolarity of pain and pleasure emerge as a central, if not core factor in investigations directly oriented to the study of mood, emotion, motivation, and temperament?

Before exploring answers to this question, it is necessary to note the difficult and not readily resolvable issues associated with grouping together constructs such as mood, emotion, motivation, and the like. Important as their distinctions may be for purposes of a fine grain analysis of the subject, they are secondary to our concerns here.

Most investigators (e.g., McNair & Lorr, 1964; Nowlis and Nowlis, 1956) who employed factor analytic methods to study mood and affect found some eight to twelve *monopolar* components as comprising the emotion spectrum. Schlosberg (1952) suggested an alternative model; in his formulation only two, ostensibly bipolar dimensions were necessary to account for all monopolar emotions, including joy, sadness, hope, anxiety, pity, elation, resentment, and delight, if they were arranged in a circular or circumplical manner. Research undertaken by Abelson and Sermat (1962), Green and Cliff (1975), Russell and Mehrabian (1977), Russell (1980), and Tellegen (1985) provide strong support for Schlosberg's thesis. Item intercorrelations in these studies are dominated by two dimensions, one clearly bipolar in form, and associated with mood orientation, termed "valences," such as pleasantness-unpleasantness, positive affect-negative affect, pleasure-displeasure. The other polar dimension represents degrees of intensity or levels of arousal, and has been arranged in antitheses such as active-quiescent, tension-sleep, excited-relaxed. In light of the seeming simplicity of the twofold circumplical model, Russell and Pratt (1980) raised the following question: If there are only two polar dimensions, could they adequately represent all of the major affective terms, such as anger, anxiety, depression, and so on, that are neither synonymous with pleasure-displeasure or with degree of arousal? After examining studies relevant to the question, Russell concluded (1980):

Indeed, many affect terms were not synonymous with (did not cluster about) the pleasantness or arousal axes. Instead, terms fell meaningfully around the perimeter of the space defined by the axes. In other words, the third property of the language of affect is that any affect word could be defined as some combination of the pleasure and arousal components (p. 1163).

It is encouraging, of course, that these two dimensions coincide precisely to the first two polarities of the evolutionary model, pleasure-pain and active-passive.

Tellegen recently undertook a series of carefully executed studies designed to obviate possible methodological confounds in earlier research (Tellegen, 1985; Watson and Tellegen, 1984; Zevon and Tellegen, 1982). His work has led him to conclude also that relationships among mood descriptors are best arranged in a two-factor circumplex, one akin to those formulated by Schlosberg, Russell, and others. Although preferring to give primary emphasis to the clearly bipolar axis he terms "positive affect" and "negative affect," as well as a bipolarity associated with "constraint," Tellegen labels as major circumplex unidimensions those of "pleasantness-unpleasantness" and "strong engagement-disengagement," the latter clustering the same adjectives which others refer to as arousal level. Tellegen's systematic work corresponds again to the first two polarities of the evolutionary model.

Of interest is the finding in several factorial and circumplical studies of a small but appreciable segment of variance that fails to be subsumed in the two polarity framework. For example, Russell and Mehrabian (1974, 1977) found evidence for a third polarity, initially labeled by them "dominance-submission." Closer examination of the terms employed in their study suggests that the polarity they uncovered may more accurately represent the antithesis of self-control versus other-control. The utility of this third polarity may be illustrated by the fact that the self versus other dimension helps to differentiate emotions such as anger and fear, which otherwise share both high arousal (activation) and low pleasure (pain); they may be distinguished by adding the self-other polarity in that anger falls high on self, and fear falls high on other. Should this third dimension be replicated in future research, it would add further to the validity of the tripartite evolutionary model.

A few words should be said about the temperament theory of Arnold Buss. In numerous articles and books, notably those with former students (e.g., Buss and Plomin, 1975, 1984), he has undertaken experiments and surveys to identify the central components of inherited and long-standing mood dispositions, i.e., temperaments. In his latest formulations Buss concludes that strong evidence can be adduced for the presence of three components of temperament: arousal, emotionality, and sociability. Although he does not arrange these into polar antitheses or a circumplical framework (e.g., active-passive for arousal, pain-pleasure for emotionality, self-other for sociability), the "temperaments" that his work has generated are in many ways isomorphic with the three polarities of the evolutionary model.

Neurobiologic Substrates of Mood

It is notable that investigations seeking to unravel the underlying biologic mechanisms of both normal and pathologic emotions uncover structures and processes that closely parallel the polarity dimensions described in the preceding section.

Eysenck (1967, 1981) was the first to propose a modern biologically anchored model of dispositions to both normal and pathological personality functioning based on levels of cortical arousal interacting with regions of autonomic and limbic system reactivity. Central to Eysenck's several theses is the bipolar distinction between positive or pleasant emotions, on the one hand, and negative or unpleasant emotions, on the other; according to his model, negative affects are associated with excessively high or low arousal levels, whereas moderate levels are more likely to be experienced as positive. As is well known, Eysenck has extended these notions to the characterization of "neurotic" versus "stable" personalities, the former disposed to experience unpleasant affects by virtue of inherent and/or learned high levels of autonomic system reactivity which potentiate "pain" centers of the limbic system. As the first major theorist favoring a clear explication of the interplay of neural substrates and experiential learning, subsequent neurobiologic theorists owe much to Eysenck's pioneering work.

Among those whose work is mostly clearly related to that of Eysenck is his former student, Gray (1981, 1982). Drawing concepts from neuroanatomy, learning theory and pharmacology, Gray formulated a neurobiologic model that centers heavily on activation and inhibition (active-passive polarities), as well as on signals of reward and punishment (pleasure-pain polarity). Basing his deductions primarily on pharmacologic investigations of animal behavior, Gray has proposed the existence of three discrete, yet interrelated and neuroanatomically grounded response systems to stimuli which activate various positive and negative affects.

Although the behavioral activation system (BAS) may more properly be conceived as a system undergirding levels of arousal rather than mood valence, Gray refers to it as an "approach system" that is subserved by the reward center uncovered originally by Olds and Milner (1954). Ostensibly mediated at brainstem and cerebellar levels, it is likely to include dopaminergic projections across various striata, and is defined as responding to *conditioned* rewarding and safety stimuli by facilitating behaviors that maximize their future recurrence (Gray, 1975). There are intricacies in the manner with which the BAS is linked to external stimuli and its anatomic substrates, but Gray currently views it as a system that subserves signals of reward, punishment relief, and pleasure. As Gray has formulated the BAS, it coalesces both the pleasantness valence with arousal intensities, a difficulty that may call for future clarification.

As for "pain" signals and emotions, Gray suggests two systems, both of which alert the organism to possible dangers in the environment. Those mediating the behavioral effects of *unconditioned* (instinctive?) aversive events are termed the fight/flight system (FFS). This system elicits defensive aggression and escape, is subserved, according to Gray's pharmacologic inferences, by the amgydala, the ventromedial hypothalamus, and the central gray of the midbrain; neurochemically, evidence suggests a difficult-to-unravel interaction among aminobutyric acids (e.g., GABA), serotonin, and endogenous opiates (e.g., endorphins).

The second major source of sensitivity and action in response to "pain" signals is referred to by Gray as the behavioral inhibition system (BIS), consisting of the interplay of the septal-hippocampal system, its cholinergic projections and monoamine transmissions to the hypothalamus, and then on to the cingulate and prefrontal cortex. Activated by signals of punishment or nonreward, the BIS presumably suppresses associated behaviors, refocuses the organism's attention, and redirects activity toward alternate stimuli.

Gray's impressive physiologic experiments and felicitous conjectures add strong evidence and substantive logic to the fundamental dichotomy of pleasure- and pain-oriented systems at the neurobiologic level. We will return to his inventive work again when we focus our attention on the passive-active polarity.

A recent neurobiologic schema that accords with the polarity model has been presented by Cloninger (1986, 1987). Drawing on family and developmental studies, personality psychometrics and, most significantly, neuropharmacologic and neuroanatomical correlates of behavioral conditioning, Cloninger has generated a theoretical model composed of three dimensions, which he terms "reward dependence," "harm avoidance," and "novelty seeking." Proposing that each is a heritable personality disposition, he relates them explicitly to specific monoaminergic pathways, for example, high reward dependence is connected to low noradrenergic activity, harm avoidance is associated with high serotonergic activity, and high novelty seeking relates to low dopaminergic activity. Although Cloninger characterizes these three dimensions in a distinctive and ingenious manner, they nonetheless appear to conform rather closely to the circumplical model of emotions and other personologic formulations that have repeatedly been described in the literature—for example, the work of Russell (1980) and Tellegen (1985) described in the previous section, as well as the proposals of Freud (1915/1925), Gray (1964, 1982), Eysenck (1967, 1981), Millon (1969, 1981), and Sjobring (1973).

To illustrate, it appears that Cloninger's reward dependence dimension reflects highs and lows on the positive-gratifying-pleasure valence, whereas the harm avoidance dimension represents highs and lows on the valence of negative-pain-displeasure. Although more relevant to the active-passive dimensional polarity, to be discussed in the next section, Cloninger's descriptive portrayal of high and low novelty seeking appears to parallel the dichotomous arousal levels on various circumplex models (e.g., engagement-energetic-active versus disengagement-quiescent-passive). We will return to this latter dichotomy in a later section, elaborating for the present the reward dependence and harm avoidance polarity.

For Cloninger, reward dependence is hypothesized to be a heritable neurobiological tendency to respond to signals of reward (pleasure), particularly verbal signals of social approval, sentiment and succor, as well as to resist events which might extinguish behaviors previously associated with these rewards. Cloninger portrays those high on reward dependence to be sociable, sympathetic, and pleasant; in contrast, those low on this polarity are characterized as detached, cool, and practical. Describing the undergirding substrate for the reward/pleasure valence as the behavior maintenance system (BMS), Cloninger speculates that its prime neuromodulator is likely to be that of norepinephrine, with its major ascending pathways arising in the pons, projecting onward to hypothalamic and limbic structures, and then branching upward to the neocortex.

Harm avoidance is seen as a heritable tendency to respond intensely to signals of aversive stimuli (pain) and to learn to inhibit behaviors which might lead to punishment and frustrative nonreward. Those high on this dimension are characterized as cautious, apprehensive and inhibited; those low on this valence would likely be confident, optimistic and carefree. Cloninger subscribes essentially to Gray's behavioral inhibition system concept in explicating this polarity, as well as the neuroanatomic and neurochemical hypotheses Gray proposed as the substrates for its "pain-avoidant" mechanisms.

There are sound reasons to approach neurobiologic speculations with a measure of skepticism, given the tenuous nature of our knowledge concerning the complexities of neurochemical interaction. Similarly, hesitation must be expressed concerning hypotheses that propose direct parallels between neurobiologic and behavior/emotion systems. Nonetheless, it should be encouraging when one encounters convergence among diverse fields of inquiry. Observing parallels to the "aims of existence," that is, the polarity of enhancing life, on the one hand, and preserving life, on the other, are especially notable in the several psychological domains in which the pleasure and pain antithesis is expressed, particularly those covered in this section; learning, unconscious processes, moods, and their neurobiologic substrates.

We turn next to a unidimensional polarity that has been alluded to time and again, that of arousal levels, a construct conceptualized within the evolutionary framework as modes of ecologic adaptation, and manifested specifically in what has been termed the passive-active polarity.

Modes of Adaptation

Ecologic Accommodation and Ecologic Modification: The Passive-Active Polarity

The evolutionary development of two primary modes by which living organisms adapt to their ecologic environments was previously described; as noted, these modes correspond closely, if somewhat imperfectly, to the evolution of the plant and animal "kingdoms." Plants best characterize the mode of ecologic *accommodation*, an essentially *passive* style which disposes them to locate and remain securely anchored in a niche where the elements comprising their environment (e.g., soil, temperature, sunlight) furnish both the nourishment and protection requisite to sustaining individual homeostatic balance and promoting species survival. Animals, in contrast, typify what has been termed adaptation via ecologic *modification*, an essentially *active* style which intervenes and transforms the surrounds, a versatile mobility that enables the organism not only to seek out its needs and to escape threats to its survival, but also to reconstruct or shift from one niche to another as unpredictable events arise.

Broadening the polarity to encompass human experience, the active-passive dimension means that the vast range of behaviors engaged in by humans may fundamentally be grouped in terms of whether initiative is taken in altering and shaping life's events or whether our behaviors are reactive and accommodate to those events. Often reflective and deliberate, those who are passively oriented manifest few overt strategies to gain their ends. This display a seeming inertness, a phlegmatic lack of ambition or persistence, a tendency toward acquiescence, a restrained attitude in which they initiate little to modify events, waiting for the circumstances of their environment to take their course before making accommodations. Some persons may be temperamentally ill-equipped to rouse or assert themselves; perhaps past experience has deprived them of opportunities to acquire a range of competencies, or confidence in their ability to master the events of their environment; equally possible is a naive confidence that things will come their way with little or no effort on their part. From a variety of diverse sources, then, those at the passive end of the polarity engage in few direct instrumental activities to intercede in events or generate the effects they desire. They seem suspended, quiescent, placid, immobile, restrained, listless, waiting for things to happen and reacting to them only after they occur.

Descriptively, those who are at the active end of the polarity are best characterized by their alertness, vigilance, liveliness, vigor, forcefulness, their stimulus-seeking energy, and drive. Some plan strategies and scan alternatives to circumvent obstacles or avoid the distress of punishment, rejection, and anxiety. Others are impulsive, precipitate, excitable, rash, and hasty, seeking to elicit pleasures and rewards. Although specific goals vary and change from time to time, actively aroused individuals intrude on passing events and energetically and busily modify the circumstances of their environment.

We should be mindful, as stated previously, that the passive-active antithesis is unidimensional; the behavior patterns of organisms may fall at various intermediary points of the continuum. It should also be recalled that the same organism (human or otherwise) varies in its levels of arousal, at times engaging vigorously its environment and, at others, resting quietly, content and relaxed within its surrounds. It should be noted as well that passivity and activity are not homogeneous constructs; they are multireferential and exhibit diverse forms of expression. The natural historian, Alexander Skutch, beautifully characterizes this diversity among plant and animal species. Portraying the varieties of ecologic modification among animals, which is proposed as the foundation of the active mode, Skutch writes (1985):

> Animals (are) thrown into relentless competition for food and living space. Some attacked the vegetation, gnawing into the foliage in the manner of many insect larvae, often until scarcely a single leaf remained intact on a great tree. Or they bored into living stems and branches, frequently killing the plant that sustained them. Among the larger animals, the grazers cropped the tender herbage in great quantities, while the browsers stripped shrubs and trees as high as they could reach. Other animals become carnivorous, striking down living victims that they tore and mangled mercilessly. Still others, usually of the smaller sorts,

adopted parasitic habits, living on or within the bodies of their hosts, sapping their strength, perhaps causing, in sum, more suffering than did carnivores that killed at a stroke (pp. 68–69).

Portraying aspects of the diverse manifestations of eco-logic accommodation among plants, which is proposed as the foundation of the passive mode, Skutch (1985) writes as follows:

Plants' competition for a place in the soil and sunlight is gentle and persistent rather than violent . . . . They never, like animals, expel other individuals from a terri-tory . . . but they tolerate members of the same or differ-ent species in closest proximity. A great diversity of plants with similar needs can thrive close together , , . . Consider the great variety of the shapes of leaves, all engaged in productive photosynthesis in the same meadow or woodland; the differences in their arrange-ment, alternate, opposite, or whorled; the various sys-tems of branching of the plants that bear them. Or contemplate the immense diversity in the structures and colors of flowers that can be pollinated by the same agents—bees, butterflies, birds or wind (pp. 57–58).

Let us turn once more, albeit briefly, to the four domains of psychological investigation we have chosen to represent each of the polarities: learned behaviors, unconscious processes, emotion, and motivation, and their biologic substrates.

Respondent versus Operant Modes of Learned Behavior

This section will be brief owing to the fairly explicit distinctions that exist between passive and active modes of learning, best illustrated in the clear separation made by B. F. Skinner in his "theoretical formulations." Skinner's exemplary work in this field enables us to maintain consistency with the previous discussion of the "reinforcers" of learning. For the present we will bypass the implicit and complex modes of learning that are attributable to the unique abstract capabilities of the human mind.

Universal among mammalian species are two basic modes of learning, the respondent or conditioned type and the operant or instrumental type. The former is essentially a *passive* process, the simple pairing of an innate or reflexive response to a stimulus which previously did not elicit that response. In like passive fashion, environmental elements which occur either simultaneously or in close temporal order become connected to each other in the organisms' repertoire of learning, such that if one of these elements recurs in the future, the expectation is that the others will follow or be elicited. Nothing active need be done by the organism to achieve these learnings; inborn reflexive responses and/or environmental events are merely associated by contiguity.

Operant or instrumental learnings, in contrast, represent the outcome of an *active* process on the part of the organism, one that requires an effort and execution on its part that has the effect of altering the environment. Whereas respondent conditioning occurs as a result of the passive observation of a conjoining of events, operant conditioning occurs only as a result of an active modification by the organism of its surroundings, a performance usually followed by a positive reinforcer (pleasure) or the successful avoidance of a negative one (pain). Unconditioned reflexes, such as a leg jerk in reaction to a knee tap, will become a passively acquired conditioned respondent if a bell is regularly sounded prior to the tap, as will the shrinking reflex of an eye pupil passively become conditioned to that bell if it regularly preceded exposure to a shining light. In contrast, a foraging bird, by virtue of its actions, will acquire an operant habit of scratching among, and uncovering ground leaves, if these efforts exposed nourishing insects and seeds. Henceforth, that bird will intentionally and busily alter surrounding ground conditions in its environment to meet periodic nutritional needs because it has learned that nourishment is contingent on actively performing particular behaviors.

In sum, the respondent-operant learning distinction appears to be a clear illustration of accommodation versus modification, as well as the passive-active polarity.

Reality Apparatuses of the Ego

Prior to the impressively burgeoning literature on "self" and "object relations" theory of the past two decades, the passive-active antithesis was given a central place in both classical "instinct" and post-World War II "ego" schools of psychoanalytic thought. The contemporary focus on "self" and "object" is considered in discussions of the third polarity, that of self-other. We have not, nor should we overlook the once key and now less "popular" constructs of both instinct theory and ego theory. It may be worth noting, as well as of special interest to the evolutionary model presented in this book, that the beginnings of psychoanalytic metapsychology were initially oriented largely to instinctual derivatives (where pleasure and pain were given prominence), progressed subsequently to the apparatuses of the ego (Hartmann, 1939; Rapaport, 1953)—where passivity and activity were centrally involved—and now, most prominently the "split," if you will, between "self" and "object" schools. As in prior sections, the intent here is neither to make explicit nor to elaborate the many intricacies of "ego apparatuses," but rather to demonstrate that a major period of analytic thought gave prominent attention to one of the three polarities of the evolutionary model, in this case that of "activity-passivity."

Freud's systematic use of the terms active and passive may first be found in his *Three Essays on the Theory of Sexuality* (1905), where he characterized them as the two kinds of aims of instinctual drives. Activity, he noted, was put into operation by the instinct for mastery, enacted through the somatic musculature; the erotogenic mucous was the organ he considered primary in representing the passive aims of the sexual instinct. Ten years later, in his metapsychology papers (1915/1925), Freud not only set forth his polarity schema, as noted previously, but described, albeit briefly, further attributes to distinguish the active-passive antithesis. To quote (Freud, 1915/1925):

> The antithesis of active and passive must not be confounded with that of ego-subject—external object. The relation of the ego to the outer world is passive in so far as it receives stimuli from it, active when it reacts to these. Its instincts compel it to a quite special degree of activity towards the outside world, so that, if we wished to emphasize the essence of the matter, we might say that the ego-subject is passive in respect of external stimuli, active in virtue of its own instincts (p. 77).

As Schafer (1968) has noted, in designating instinctual aims as active or passive Freud does not refer to aims as ends or goals, but rather as instrumentalities, or what Hartmann (1939) termed the ego apparatuses. The ends or goals of an aim, according to Schafer are (1968):

> . . . In this context, aim does refer to one aspect of the means or mode used to achieve an instinctual end: the aim is *active* if its gratification depends on the subjects acting on an object; the aim is *passive* if its gratification depends on the objects acting on the subject (pp. 173–174).

To paraphrase the preceding in terms of the evolutionary model, active signifies the modification of an environment, whereas passive signifies an accommodation to the environment.

Rapaport (1953) carries this theme further in a theoretical discussion relating intrapsychic structures such as ego and id. The *model of activity*, as he puts it, is a dual one; first, the ego is strong enough to defend against or control the intensity of the id's drive tensions or, second, through the competence and energy of its apparatuses, the ego is successful in uncovering or creating in reality the object of the id's instinctual drives. Rapaport conceives the *model of passivity* also to be a dual one; first, either the ego gradually modulates or indirectly discharges the instinctual energies of the id, or, second, lacking an adequately controlling apparatus is rendered powerless and subject thereby to instinctual forces. Translating these formulations into evolutionary terms, effective actions by the ego will successfully manage the internal forces of the id, whereas passivity will result either in accommodations or, exposure to the internal demands of the id.

In addition to its utility in explicating the *aims* of instinctual drives, and in portraying the interaction between intrapsychic *structures*, the active-passive antithesis is employed also in the psychoanalytic characterization of *object relations*. To quote Schafer (1968):

> Clinicians are accustomed to say of people that they are either generally active or passive in their relationships or typically so in certain kinds of relationships. When they say a person is passive, they usually imply dependency upon others, helplessness, a lack of initiative, predominant receptiveness, and perhaps a demanding personality. At times when they use the term passive they also imply feminine; at other times they imply orality or anality. The opposites of most of these terms are implied when they say a person is active in his relationships (p. 179).

Low and High Intensities of Activation

Much has been said on this topic in a previous section describing factorial studies and circumplical models of reported and expressed moods. As noted, two major dimensions or polarities emerge repeatedly. Specifically, the first dimension is best arranged along a continuum with terms such as elated, pleased, and happy, at one end, and miserable, sad, and distressed, at the other. The second continuum essentially represents levels of activation, or degrees of motivation, a spread of emotive intensity ranging from excited, alarmed, and astonished, at one extreme, to tired, bored, and sleepy, at the other. In characterizing their formulation of "mood structure," Watson and Tellegen (1984) note: "the high end of each dimension represents a state of emotional arousal (or high affect), whereas the low end of each factor is most clearly and strongly defined by terms reflecting a relative absence of affective involvement" (p. 221).

It should be recalled that many an early investigator followed the line of reasoning put forth by Walter Cannon (1927, 1939), the great neurophysiologist of the early 1920s and 1930s. He asserted that moods and emotions were essentially variations of energized behavior, that identical visceral changes undergirded a variety of diverse motivational states, and that the underlying physiology of different affects merely signified lesser or greater levels of a general state of arousal. So conceived, mood and motivational states were not comprised of two or more discrete emotions (even those of pleasure and pain), but merely expressed different magnitudes of a single, quantitative dimension of brain activation. This view was not at variance with the formulations originally proposed by Pavlov on the key role he assigned CNS (central nervous system) excitation, nor was it inconsistent with Freud's conviction that increases and decreases in drive tension determined much of the character of emotional states.

As seems evident from contemporary research, the construct of activation/arousal is a principal and necessary component in describing mood/motivation states. Animator and energizer of both behavior and emotion, it combines either with the direction of behavior, that is, the dimension of approach-avoidance as Duffy (1957), Lindsley (1951), and Schneirla (1959) have put it, or the valence of emotions, that is, the dimension of pleasure-pain, as we, Russell (1980), Schlosberg (1952), and Tellegen (1985), have put it.

Interest here is not on elaborating or explicating the varieties and intricacies of the active-passive dimension, but rather to provide a foundation for affirming its place as a substantive construct in the domain of psychological thought. Nevertheless, a word or two is called for in recording features that differentiate activity-passivity beyond merely signifying levels of energy. Among the more notable secondary concepts of activation are those of *threshold*—that is, the ease with which one can be roused to respond to stimuli or to expend energy— and *rhythmicity*—that is, cycles or consistencies in activity level, such as evincing an unchanging or fixed intensity, as opposed to being labile and unpredictable (Millon, 1969).

Little more need be said concerning the concept of arousal level other than the observation that it essentially a unidimensional construct that conforms closely to the evolutionary polarity of activity-passivity.

Neurobiological Substrates of Arousal

Neurobiological research has proven to be highly supportive of the arousal construct ever since Papez (1937), Moruzzi and Magoun (1949) and MacLean (1949, 1952) assigned what were to be termed the reticular and limbic systems' both energizing and expressive roles in the CNS; as noted in a prior section, it is the limbic system and the higher cortical centers which appear to integrate, differentiate, and elaborate the character and valence of emotion/motivation.

In exploring how the substrates of emotion and arousal interact to form clinically relevant disorders, we travel well beyond established proximal mechanisms to extremely speculative realms. Little need be said of the basics of autonomic and central nervous processes in a chapter such as this; more, if not much more, is called for concerning how some of the more notable past and current theorists and investigators have employed the arousal construct to form clinical derivatives. We will make an attempt, albeit, brief.

First among historic figures to undertake this task was Ivan Pavlov. In speaking of the basic properties of the nervous system, Pavlov referred to the *strength* of the processes of *excitation* and *inhibition*, the *equilibrium* between their respective strengths, as well as the *mobility* of nervous processes. Although Pavlov's theoretical formulations (1927) dealt with what Donald Hebb (1955) termed a "conceptual nervous system," his experiments and those of his students led to innumerable direct investigations of brain activity. Central to Pavlov's thesis was the distinction between *strong* and *weak* types of nervous system. In a synopsis of Pavlov's conceptions, Gray states (1964):

> . . . the weak nervous system was said to be more "sensitive," less "stable," and more "excitable" than the strong; it was said that "the strong nervous system acts as if it damped down stimulation, while the weak nervous system acts as if it amplified it. A more fashionable way of making the same distinction would be to say that the weak nervous system is more easily or more highly "aroused"; and the personality dimension known as "strength of the nervous system" could be described as a dimension of "levels of arousal" or of "arousability" (p. 289).

Numerous students of Pavlov developed personality and temperament typologies employing his basic concepts of excitation-inhibition, strength-weakness, mobility, a set of unidimensional polarities that possess features with superficial similarities to the evolutionary model formulated in this chapter. Teplov (1961) and his student Nebylitsyn (1969), as well as Ivanov-Smolenski (1953), Krasnogorsky (1954) and Strelau (1983) each have generated clinically-related typologies that accord most closely with the four temperaments of the ancient Greeks, namely sanguine, phlegmatic, choleric, and melancholic. There are well-grounded neurophysiologic and electroencephalographic bases for these conceptions, but details concerning them would take us too far afield.

Although extrapolations of a worthy nature employing or analyzing data related to the substrates of arousal have been promulgated by Western investigators in the 1950s and 1960s, such as Eysenck (1967), Hebb (1949), and Lindsley (1951), we will bypass them also, limiting our brief discussion to more contemporary theorists such as Gray (1982) and Cloninger (1987).

In describing his interpretation of arousability, Gray focuses on the role of the reticular activating system of the brain stem. To him, level of arousal is a function of the degree to which the cerebral cortex is bombarded by impulses from the nonspecific reticular system, the bombardment itself being a function of both the intensity and the novelty of stimuli generated either from external or internal sources. No less important are individual differences in arousability: specifically, those who are low on this dimension are considered to possess a strong nervous system, whereas those who are high are referred to as possessing a weak nervous system. Closely aligned to modern variants of Pavlovian theory, Gray would be inclined to agree that those with weak nervous systems are easily aroused, nonsensation seeking introverts who would experience low stimulation preferable to high levels. Conversely, those with strong nervous systems would arouse easily, be likely to be sensation-seeking extroverts who find low stimulation levels to be boring and high levels to be both exciting and pleasant.

The work of Zuckerman (1979) on sensation-seeking provides a major empirical bridge connecting the theoretical schemas of Pavlov and his students, as well as those of Eysenck and his former student, Gray, but it is Cloninger (1986, 1987) who has recently extracted the concept of "novelty-seeking" from the matrix of studies and conjectures surrounding the arousal construct; in so doing, he has provided an inventive if speculative neurobiologic thesis to serve as its substrate.

To Cloninger, novelty-seeking is a heritable tendency toward excitement in response to novel stimuli or cues for reward (pleasure) or punishment (pain) relief which leads to frequent exploratory activity. Consonant with its correspondence to the arousal dimension, individuals who are assumed to be high in novelty-seeking are characterized as impulsive, exploratory, excitable, as well as quickly distracted or bored. Conversely, those at the passive or low end of the novelty-seeking dimension are portrayed by Cloninger as reflective, stoic, slow-tempered, orderly, and only slowly engaged in new interests.

Our interpretation of Cloninger's concept of novelty-seeking would place it squarely in the realm of arousal/ activation; in this regard it shares some of the difficulties to which we alluded previously in noting the mixed valence and arousal character of Gray's behavior activation system (BAS). In fact, Cloninger himself refers to individual differences in the novelty-seeking tendency as reflecting variations in the BAS. Though the term novelty-seeking suggests a valence toward pleasurable stimuli, Cloninger includes within its behavioral scope the "active avoidance or escape from potential punishment."

Nonetheless, Cloninger (1987) does elaborate on some of Gray's well-reasoned, if speculative, conjectures concerning the neurobiologic mechanisms of the BAS and novelty-seeking constructs:

> . . . Dopaminergic cell bodies in the midbrain receive inputs from several sources and then project impulses to the forebrain, thereby acting as the final common pathway for the behavioral activation system . . . . Such behavioral activation is associated with a particular pattern of physiological arousal, particularly an increased heart rate and decreased sensation threshold.

In mammals, dopaminergic projections to the forebrain play a central role in these functions via . . . projections . . . to limbic structures . . . and mesofrontal projections . . . . Inputs to the dopaminergic cell bodies include ascending paths in the reticular formation, descending paths from the hypothalamus, and feedback from the cerebral cortex via the amygdala and caudate (p. 575).

Strategies of Replication

Reproductive Propagation and Reproductive Nurturance: The Self-Other Polarity

As described earlier, recombinant replication achieved by sexual mating entails a balanced though asymmetric parental investment in both the genesis and nurturance of offspring. By virtue of her small number of eggs and extended pregnancy, the female strategy for replicative success that has evolved among most mammals is characterized by the intensive care and protection of a limited number of offspring. Oriented to reproductive nurturance rather than reproductive propagation, most adult females, at least until recent decades in Western society, bred close to the limit of their capacity, attaining a reproductive ceiling of approximately 20 viable births. By contrast, not only are males free of the unproductive pregnancy interlude for mating, but may substantially increase their reproductive output by engaging in repetitive matings with as many available females as possible. Although most human societies are organized to optimize a balance between genders in mating, nurturance, and protection, the male animal is biologically capable of following the *r*-strategy of maximizing self-propagation by profligate breeding, whereas the female of the species adheres more closely to the *K*-strategy of intensively nurturing and thereby enhancing the survival of her few offspring. As noted previously, it is my contention that a crucial consequence flows from these disparate replication strategies.

Males tend to be *self-oriented* owing to the fact that competitive advantages that inhere within themselves maximize the replication of their genes. Conversely, females tend to be *other-oriented* owing to the fact that their competence in nurturing and protecting their limited progeny maximize the replication of their genes.

The self versus other antithesis follows from other aspects of evolution's asymmetric replication strategy. Not only must the female be oriented to and vigilant in identifying the needs of and dangers that may face each of her few offspring, but it is reproductively advantageous for the female to be sensitive to and discriminating in her assessment of potential mates. A "bad" mating, i.e., one which issues a defective or weak offspring, has more grave consequences for the female than for the male. Not only will such an event appreciably reduce her limited reproductive possibilities, as well as foregoing a better mate for a period of time, but she may exhaust much of her nurturing and protective energies in her attempts to revitalize an inviable or infertile offspring. By contrast, if a male indulges in a "bad" mating, all he has lost are some quickly replaceable sperm, a loss that will do little to diminish his future reproductive potentials and activities.

Before we turn to the expression of the self-other polarity in diverse psychological domains remember that the conceptually derived extremes articulated in the form of the self-other polarity do not evince themselves in sharp and distinct "reality" differences. Gender-related proclivities, for example, are matters of degree, not absolutes, a fact owing not only to the consequences of recombinant "shuffling" and gene "crossing over," but to the influential effects of cultural values and social learning. Consequently, most individuals exhibit intermediate characteristics on this, as well as on other polarities. The evolutionary roots of this polarity do manifest themselves in modest *group* differences between the genders, however, an observation to be considered again later.

Internal Versus External Controls of Learning

As in a number of concepts discussed previously, constructs such as self and other are not only multireferential, but are typically represented by diverse terminologies, each of which highlight different facets of the core construct. Thus, dimensions labeled internal-external, ego-object, self-nonself, or independent-dependent, to name a few, may be aspects or be derivations of the self-other polarity, each giving prominence to features more suitable or more precise in the context or subject domain within which they are employed.

In the domain of learned behaviors, the parallel most consonant with the self-other polarity is Rotter's construct of "locus of control," more particularly the antithesis he proposed between internal and external loci of reinforcement control. Rotter formulated his thesis as follows (1966):

> . . . an event regarded by some persons as a reward or reinforcement may be differently perceived and reacted to by others. One of the determinants of this reaction is the degree to which the individual perceives that the reward follows from, or is contingent upon, his own behavior or attributes versus the degree to which he feels the reward is controlled by forces outside himself and may occur independently of his own actions . . . . When a reinforcement is perceived by the subject as following some action of his own but not being entirely contingent upon his action, then . . . it is typically perceived as . . . under the control of . . . other . . . . When the event is interpreted in this way by an individual, we

have labeled this a belief in *external control*. If the person perceives that the event is contingent upon his own behavior . . . we have termed this a belief in *internal control*.

It is hypothesized that this variable is of major significance in understanding the nature of learning processes . . . and also that consistent individual differences exist among individuals. (p. 1)

Rotter's formulation partially fuses self versus other locus with activity-passivity, as was the proposal of Angyal (1941), who considered a crucial difference among individuals to be the degree to which they sought to make themselves "master" of their environment versus permitting the environment to be master of them. White's (1959) concept of *competence* likewise relates to the sphere of effective functioning, suggesting an implicit dimension in which individuals differ in the extent to which self-efficacy in one's environment takes precedence over forces within the environment.

Of note also are the recent views of erstwhile behaviorists who have broken from their former exclusive focus on external controls of reinforcement (stimuli, events, others) by giving primacy to the role of what they have termed self-reinforcers. Bandura (1977) typifies this signal shift in stressing the role of the self-system. In the following quote he points out why it is improbable that all behaviors can be controlled exclusively by external events (Bandura, 1977):

If actions were determined solely by external rewards and punishments, people would behave like weather-vanes, constantly shifting in different directions to conform to the momentary influences impinging upon them (p. 128).

Bandura has not stressed differences among individuals in their receptivity to external versus self reinforcement, but others have made these variations central to their work. e.g., Rotter, Witkin.

Whether self or "nonself" is the primary source of influence was the major theme of Witkin's programmatic studies in "individual differentiation" (1954, 1977); particularly relevant are those projects which he termed *field dependence* versus *field independence*. Summarizing the results of these investigations, Witkin and Goodenough wrote, (1977):

> One of the main features of psychological differentiation is segregation of self from nonself. Self-nonself segregation means that boundaries have been formed between inner and outer . . . . Differences in degree of self-nonself segregation lead to differences in the extent to which the self, or alternatively, the field outside is likely to be used as a referent for behavior. The tendencies to rely on self or field as primary referents are the field-independent and field-dependent   styles.

> Field-dependent people make greater use of external social referents; . . . field-independent people function with greater autonomy under such conditions. Field-dependent people are more attentive to social cues than are field-independent people. Field-dependent people have an interpersonal orientation: They show strong interest in others, prefer to be physically close to people, are emotionally open, and gravitate toward social situations. Self-independent people have an impersonal orientation: They are not very interested in others, show both physical and psychological distancing from others, and prefer nonsocial situations . . . . This pattern suggests that, with regard to level, the field-dependence-independence dimension is bipolar (p. 661).

Self-Structures Versus Object Relations

The development of psychoanalytic theory has progressed, through three periods, each of which, as we conceive it, parallels one of the three antitheses proposed by Freud as "governing all of mental life"; this progression also exhibits a high degree of consonance with the three evolutionary polarities formulated in this text. Each period is dominated by one or two major constructs. The first years of psychoanalytic thought were guided by the discovery of, and preeminence given to the instinctual aims and transformations of the "id"; the constructs of this phase parallel the elemental drive characteristics and basic survival goals that comprise the evolutionary polarity of pleasure-pain. The second phase in the emergence of analytic theory was noted by the central role assigned the reality-oriented apparatuses of the "ego," the recognition that a series of regulatory mechanisms were operative in which otherwise forbidden impulses could be modulated and expressed, as well as intrapsychic conflicts managed and resolved; the constructs of this phase of psychoanalysis parallel the adaptive modes of environmental "modification" and "accommodation" that comprise the evolutionary polarity of active-passive. The third generation of psychoanalytic thought will be addressed in this section. Here, we see the emergence of the current schools of "self" versus "object relations" theory, a split in analytic orientations which recognizes the importance of personal identity and cohesion as a core theme, on the one hand, and that of internalized and enduring representations of early relationships on the other; the two prime constructs of this most recent phase of psychoanalysis parallels the strategies of self-propagation and other-nurturance that express the human dimensions of the third, or replication polarity of the evolutionary model, that portrayed by the antithesis of self-other.

A year prior to outlining his concept of three polarities, Freud (1914) formulated two directions of early libidinal object choice, the so-called anaclitic and narcissistic. The former undergirds the development of affectionate and need-satisfying relationships with the external world or "objects," whereas the latter refers to the focusing on "self" as the cathected choice. Those whose early experiences are developmentally constructive progress through a dialectic balance between the two; problematic consequences, however, can follow either progression. For Anna Freud (1965), a troubled anaclitic course leads to poorly integrated or unstable object relations. Failures in what she terms the introjective (narcissistic) developmental line result in an unconsolidated or undifferentiated sense of self or identity.

The importance of "object-relations" theory (Fairbairn, 1954; Kernberg, 1976, 1980; Klein, 1952) in expanding the frontiers of modern psychoanalytic thought cannot be overstated. Nor can the recent emergence of "self" theory (Goldberg, 1978, 1985; Kohut, 1971, 1977) be underestimated as a reinvigorating perspective. As Blatt and Shichman have put it (1983): "Self-definition and interpersonal relatedness are part of the processes often discussed as the development of the concept of the self and the object world . . . . Disruptions of (their) developmental lines . . . define two primary configurations of personality and psychopathology" (p. 200).

An early forerunner of many contemporary analytic theorists, Edith Jacobson (1964), sought to bridge the central constructs of "ego" psychology with those of "self" and "object relations." In Jacobson's metapsychology, the infant's experiences of pleasure (gratification) and displeasure (frustration) with its mother lies at the core of its subsequent conceptions of the external world. These pleasure/unpleasure experiences accrue a foundation of images of good (gratifying) and bad (frustrating) external objects which remain embedded within the infant's psyche, both as an orientation to and as a structural basis for future relationships, on the one hand, and one's sense of self, on the other. Jacobson retained the ego-analytic view of the self as an image, comparable to other images formed of external objects, rather than a "mental system," such as the ego which possesses its own psychic apparatus. Nevertheless, she assigned attributes to the self construct that were more substantial than those of other images, exploring its course and vicissitudes, its relationships with external objects, and the influences it contributed to the development of both the ego and superego.

Despite efforts to synthesize self and object constructs, as put forth in Jacobson's proposals, contemporary analytic theory has followed a more-or-less schismatic course that has separated "self-being" from "other-relating," a division seen most clearly in the divergent conceptions of Otto Kernberg and Heinz Kohut. Elaborating their respective formulations is both impractical in a chapter of this length and nature, as well as unnecessary if we wish only to record the separate roles assigned self and other in contemporary analytic thought. A paragraph or two will suffice.

Kernberg adheres closely to Jacobson's views, although he clearly characterizes his work as falling within the framework of an object relations theory. Parallels to Jacobson may be seen in the following quotes, where Kernberg writes (1976):

> . . . the buildup of dyadic or bipolar intrapsychic representations (self and object-images) are reflections of the original infant-mother relationship and its later development into dyadic, triangular and multiple internal and external interpersonal relationships (p. 57).

In Kernberg's metapsychology, the primary structures of the mind, comprising internal representations of self and others, are forged from relationship experiences, especially those imbued with instinctual affects of pleasure and displeasure. Future difficulties arise from unfused or contradictory representations of self and others, particularly when the good (pleasurable) or bad (unpleasurable) components of an inherently complex and normally coherent image have been "split" into separate representations. It is the defensive misattribution of sectors of self and others that results in the growing fragmentation of the developing child's inner world, manifesting itself in disorders such as "borderline organization" and "narcissistic personality."

To state that Kohut's theoretical model stands in clear contrast to that of Kernberg is to do an injustice to both. Each theorist, as with Jacobson and others before them, takes special care to intertwine the development of self and object relations. Differences in the eyes of dispassionate viewers are matters of emphasis; by contrast, each theorist's respective acolytes consider them fundamental, if not crucial, to understanding their common subject domains. What distinguishes Kohut from Kernberg is the emphasis Kohut gives to the continuity and cohesiveness of the phenomenologic emergence of self. Differing from those whose focus is on relationships with external objects, Kohut gives primacy not to relationships per se, but to the manner in which they affect the experience of self. Neurotic and character problems, most notably narcissistic disorders, are not the outcropping of internalized relational difficulties, but stem from failures in the environment to provide the reflective empathy necessary to develop an integrated self. Distorted or inhibited in this manner, the defective self will, as a secondary consequence, be unable to maintain mature and equalitarian ties with others. Depending on the character and timing with which a child's psychic equilibrium was undermined, he will employ various splitting and displacing operations to protect against self fragmentation, or will seek to forestall either total depletion or psychic disintegration.

Competitive Versus Cooperative Dispositions of Motivation

Toward what end are emotions oriented? To be more specific, do they serve particular functions or goals that enhance organismic survivability? An answer consonant with the evolutionary model presented in this book would state that emotions are adaptive, that their presence owes much to their effectiveness in enhancing and preserving life, that despite the fact that they can go awry by virtue of biologic defects or maladaptive learning, they fundamentally strengthen the probability of organismic viability.

Rather than discuss the valences of emotion or motivation—that is, those affects tied closely to unalloyed pleasure and pain—attention will be directed to the more complex motives and emotions and the ends to which they are disposed. Specifically, and in line with the focus of this section, that pertaining to the strategies of replication, we will attempt to show that the mixtures of different emotions, and the behaviors and cognitions with which they are interrelated, serve to enhance either or both self-propagation and other-nurturance. These more complex blends take the form of psychological constructs such as competition, aggression, altruism, cooperation, and so on; it is these to which we will turn, with the intent, as before, of demonstrating the utility of conceiving them along the dimension of self versus other.

The reasoning behind different replication strategies derives from the concept of *inclusive fitness*, the logic of which we owe to the theoretical biologist W. D. Hamilton (1964). The concept's rationale is well articulated in the following quote (Daly and Wilson, 1978):

> Suppose a particular gene somehow disposes its bearers to help their siblings. Any child of a parent that has this gene has a one-half probability of carrying that same gene by virtue of common descent from the same parent bearer . . . . From the gene's point of view, it is as useful to help a brother or sister as it is to help the child.
>
> When we assess the fitness of a . . . bit of behavior, we must consider more than the reproductive consequences for the individual animal. We must also consider whether the reproductive prospects of any kin are in any way altered. *Inclusive fitness is a sum of the consequences for one's own reproduction, plus the consequences for the reproduction of kin* multiplied by the degree of relatedness of those kin (italics added).
>
> An animal's behavior can therefore be said to serve a *strategy* whose goal is the maximization of inclusive fitness (pp. 30–31).

Although the dimension of self-other is arranged to highlight its polar extremes, it should be evident that many, if not most "strategies" are employed to achieve the goals of both self and kin reproduction. Both ends are often simultaneously achieved; at other times one may predominate. The behaviors comprising these strategies are "driven," so to speak, by a blend of arousal and mood or emotion—that is, combinations arising from intermediary positions reflecting both the life enhancement and life preservation polarity of pleasure-pain, interwoven with similar intermediary positions on the ecologic accommodation and ecologic modification polarity of activity-passivity. Phrasing "replication strategies" in terms of the abstruse and metaphorical constructs that we have does not obscure them, but rather sets this third polarity on the deeper foundations of existence and adaptation, foundations composed of the first two polarities previously described.

As you read the following paragraphs on emotion and arousal-driven behaviors that typify self and other reproductive strategies, bear in mind that these behaviors are multipurposive, that is, fulfill several functions simultaneously. To employ an analogy suggested by Daly and Wilson (1978), most strategic activities are "economic," that is, are budgeted to achieve several diverse goals. Individual differences must be considered. Some persons "invest" their time and energy in seeking shelter and protection; others are more inclined to invest their efforts in "advertising" for a mate. The ultimate "pay off" is inclusive fitness, that is, maximizing the representation of one's genes in future gene pools.

With the preceding considerations in mind, let us briefly describe two broad patterns of emotion-driven strategic behaviors, the first oriented primarily to strengthening the fitness of "self," the second to the enhanced fitness of "others," i.e., kin. We will select two among several terms to represent the complex character of these fitness strategies, namely *competition* for the "self" and *cooperation* for the "others." Competition, as applied in this context, encompasses psychological and etho-

logical constructs such as aggression, predation, and territoriality. Cooperation subsumes a number of less clearly
aligned constructs, such as altruism, sociality, and affiliation.

Although seen most clearly in the behavior of lower species, a paragraph or two elaborating the contrast between cooperation and competition and between self and other in the
spheres of cognitive and interpersonal functioning recorded in
complex human domains may also be of interest in illustrating
this third polarity of the evolutionary model. For example, interpersonal behavior styles have been organized in circumplical
models to represent a variety of dimensions, traits, and types
(Benjamin, 1974, 1986; Foa and Foa, 1974; Kiesler 1986;
Leary, 1957; Plutchik and Conte, 1985; and Wiggins, 1982).
The primary polarities that emerge vary from theorist to
theorist, but a not uncommon theme is the dimension of
dominance/competitiveness versus submissive/defensiveness.
If one analyzes the items that comprise these models one would
not be unreasonable to frame this dimension in accord with
the self-other antithesis. In fact, both Foa and Foa (1974) and
Benjamin (1974) employ the self and other terms as primary
concepts for differentiating their trait-descriptive categories.

As for cognitive styles, Beck et al (1988) has recently proposed that a major distinction be drawn between two dimensions, labeled *individuality* and *sociality*, which dispose persons to exhibit contrasting cognitive distortions. As Beck
conceives it, *individuality* characterizes persons who exhibit
an exclusive investment in themselves, who seek to control
their environment, attempt to forestall encroachments on their
private domains, display a preference for self-reliance, and seek
the power to do what they wish. By contrast, *sociality* characterizes persons who possess attitudes and goals that draw
them to others, who depend on these relationships, and who
gain satisfaction from interpersonal interactions that involve
intimacy, sharing and protection.

Turning to more basic mechanisms, Barash interprets
behaviors in accord with a sociobiologic thesis, explicating the
competitive strategy as follows (1977):

. . . maximization of personal, inclusive fitness often
involves asserting one's self at the *expense* of friends,
neighbors, and even relatives. So long as individuals
are genetically distinct, they can be expected to look out
primarily for their own best interests.

Competition occurs when two or more individuals seek
access to a resource that is somehow important to the
fitness of each and that is restricted in abundance . . .
e.g., few animals ever compete for air. However, severe
competition may erupt over food, water, nesting sites,
and/or appropriate mates (p. 209).

Barash elaborates further by stating that the aggression
construct represents the proximal mechanism of competition.
Although kin-fitness is often the spur for aggressive group
acts, both aggressive displays and aggressive behaviors are
activated primarily to protect or enhance self-fitness exhibited
either to resist the loss of an important resource, or to induce
others to surrender access to a fitness-enhancing resource.
Territoriality is likewise characterized as an emotion-driven
competitive act, one oriented to restrict population density in
regions containing resources that increase the inclusive fitness
of the individual and/or his or her kinship group, for example,
a desirable food supply, defending against predator attacks,
facilitating or maintaining mating bonds, protecting offspring
shelters, asserting reproductive dominance in a hierarchical
group, and so on.

Cooperation represents efforts leading to reciprocal "fittedness," a behavioral pattern consonant with Darwin's fundamental notions. Altruism, however, is a form of behavior in
which there is denial of self for the benefit of others, a behavioral pattern acknowledged by Darwin himself as seemingly
inconsistent with his theory (1871, p. 130). A simple extrapolation from natural selection suggests that those disposed to
engage in self-sacrifice would ultimately leave fewer and fewer
descendants; as a consequence, organisms motivated by "self-

benefitting" genes would prevail over those motivated by "other-benefitting" genes, a result leading to the eventual extinction of genes oriented to the welfare of others. Wilson, the distinguished sociobiologist states the problem directly: "How then does altruism persist?" (1978, p. 153). An entymologist of note, Wilson had no hesitation in claiming that altruism not only persists, but is of paramount significance in the lives of social insects. In accord with his sociobiologic thesis, Wilson illustrates the presence of altruism in animals as diverse as birds, deer, porpoises, and chimpanzees, who evince behaviors quite regularly such as food sharing and mutual defense in their natural settings—for example, to protect their colony's hives bees enact behaviors that lead invariably to their death.

Two underlying mechanisms have been proposed to account for cooperative behaviors such as altruism. One derives from the concept of *inclusive fitness*, briefly described in preceding paragraphs; Wilson (1978) terms this form of cooperative behavior as "hard-core" altruism, by which he means that the act is "unilaterally directed" for the benefit of others, and that the bestower neither expects nor expresses a desire for a comparable return. Following the line of reasoning originally formulated by Hamilton (1964), J. P. Rushton, a controversial Canadian researcher who has carried out illuminating r-K-strategy studies of human behavior, explicates this mechanism as follows (1984):

> . . . individuals behave so as to maximize their inclusive fitness rather than only their individual fitness; they maximize the production of successful offspring by both themselves and their relatives . . . . Social ants, for example, are one of the most altruistic species so far discovered. The self-sacrificing, sterile worker and soldier ants . . . share 75% of their genes with their sisters and so by devoting their entire existence to the needs of others . . . they help to propagate their own genes (p. 6).

The second rationale proposed as the mechanism underlying other-oriented and cooperative behaviors is termed by

Wilson as "soft-core" altruism to represent his belief that the bestower's actions are ultimately self-serving. The original line of reasoning here stems from Triver's (1971) notion of *reciprocity*, a thesis suggesting that genetically based dispositions to cooperative behavior can be explained without requiring the assumption of kinship relatedness. All that is necessary is that the performance of cooperative acts be mutual, that is, result in concurrent or subsequent behaviors which are comparably beneficial in terms of enhancing the original bestower's survivability and/or reproductive fertility.

Wilson's conclusion that the self-other dimension is a bedrock of evolutionary theory is worth quoting (1978):

> In order to understand this idea more clearly, return with me for a moment to the basic theory of evolution. Imagine a spectrum of self-serving behavior. At one extreme only the individual is meant to benefit, then the nuclear family, next the extended family (including cousins, grandparents, and others who might play a role in kin selection), then the band, the tribe, chiefdoms, and finally, at the other extreme, the highest sociopolitical units . . . . In sharks natural selection occurs overwhelmingly at the individual level; all behavior is self-centered and exquisitely appropriate to the welfare of one shark and its immediate offspring. In the Portuguese man-of-war and other . . . jellyfish that consist of great masses of highly coordinated individuals, the unit of selection is almost exclusively the colony.
>
> Human beings obviously occupy a position on the spectrum somewhere between the two extremes. (p. 158).

I note further that humans differ among themselves in their location on this spectrum, and one element that contributes to these differences is linked to gender. Thus, Wilson's statement can be amended to suggest that one gender is motivationally and emotionally more disposed to act closer to the self-serving end of the spectrum, whereas the other is inclined more toward the other-serving extreme. As stated earlier, the two genders differ in terms of *group averages*, and *not* necessarily as individuals.

Neurobiological Substrates of Gender

Where will we find the proximal neurobiologic underpinnings that subserve the self versus other polarity? The answer, in our view, is that evolutionary logic points to gender differences associated with mating patterns and parental investments. In light of this assertion, and to avoid misinterpretations, a point raised earlier should be restated. What is being addressed in this and parallel sections relates *not* to gender per se, but to its connection to a crucial polarity distinction in the evolutionary model, that of self-centeredness versus other-centeredness, to phrase it anew. There are data to support this distinction in the literature, to which we will refer shortly, but this polarity's association with gender is a deduction from evolutionary thinking. The relation to gender is far from a perfect or clear-cut one. Although the comparisons drawn between genders are real they are presented here to highlight and contrast two modes of human relatedness. Moreover, where differences in gender exist they are often as much a function of social roles and cultural traditions as they are of the evolved mechanisms of reproductive biology. Reflections on this thorny subject have led us to formulate a general developmental principle (Millon, 1969): Initial constitutional differences, however, small, tend to be accentuated by social experience and cultural reinforcement. For example, a youngster with natural athletic talents will be encouraged to engage in athletic activities; these experiences are likely to be more extensive and intensive than those of an average youngster, thereby nurturing the already talented youngster's athletic skills further and, hence, enhancing comparative abilities. One further disclaimer: It is often a touchy affair when writing about racial or gender matters, particularly when such topics often are seen to imply judgments of "better" or "worse." Interpretations of this nature cannot be drawn regarding different evolutionary strategies because self- and other-oriented strategies are not only reciprocally necessary, but both have met the ultimate and only test that counts in evolution, that of having survived.

Intriguing data and ideas have been proposed by several researchers seeking to identify specific substrates which may relate to the other-oriented and self-oriented polarities. In what has been termed the affiliation/attachment drive, Everly (1988), for example, provides evidence favoring an anatomic role for the cingulate gyrus. Referring to the work of Henry and Stephens (1977), MacLean (1985), and Steklis and Kling (1985), Everly concludes that the ablation of the cingulate eliminates both affiliative and grooming behaviors. The proximal physiology of this drive has been hypothesized as including serotonergic, noradrenergic, and opoid neurotransmission systems (Everly, 1988; Redmond, Maas, and Kling, 1971). MacLean (1985) has argued that the affiliative drive may be phylogenically coded in the limbic system, and may undergird the "concept of family" in primates. The drive toward other-oriented behaviors, such as attachment, nurturing, affection, reliability, and collaborative play, has been referred to as the "cement of society" by Henry and Stevens (1977).

At the self-oriented pole, Everly proposes an autonomy/aggression substrate that manifests itself in a strong need for control and domination, as well as in hierarchical status striving. According to MacLean (1986), it appears that the amygdaloid complex may play a key role in orienting organisms to self-preservation behaviors. Early studies of animals with ablated amygdalas showed a notable increase in their docility (Kluver and Bucy, 1939), as have nonhuman primates exhibited significant decreases in social hierarchical status (Pribram, 1962). Although the evidence remains somewhat equivocal, norepinephrine and dopamine seem to be the prime neurotransmitters of this drive, as does the testosterone hormone appear similarly implicated (Feldman and Quenzar, 1984).

Turning from concrete neurobiologic substrates, much is owed to Carol Gilligan for her astute and sensitively written book *In a Different Voice* (1982). Professor Gilligan has not only effectively and forthrightly argued the case for reinterpreting psychological development in a more balanced fashion than in the past, where male values and roles are depicted as the standard, but she has lucidly portrayed distinctions which lie at the heart of gender differences. Summarizing one aspect of Gilligan's wide-ranging thesis, the sociobiologist Barash writes as follows (1986):

> . . . success is likely to be achieved somewhat differently among the two sexes. Male success is typically achieved by effective competition; female success, by relationship, especially with their own offspring and other relatives. Thus, for boys and men, morality is at its most ideal and alluring when it is a morality of justice, of theoretical principles that place restraints upon aggressive, competitive, self-serving tendencies; for girls and women, on the other hand, morality is suffused with images of relationship, of caring, and of taking care of others (p. 110).

Although Gilligan is not loathe to ascribe the origins of these differences to biological properties, she gives special attention to contrasting aspects of the developmental experiences of the two genders. Drawing on a line of reasoning first argued by Horney (1926/1967) in criticizing Freud's androcentric bias, and carried forward by Mead (1949), Lynn (1961), and most recently by Chodorow (1974, 1978), Gilligan, in her elegant expressive style, presents this thesis as follows (1982):

> . . . relationships, and particularly issues of dependency, are experienced differently by women and men. For boys and men, separation and individuation are critically tied to gender identity since separation from the mother is essential for the development of masculinity.

For girls and women, issues of femininity or feminine identity do not depend on the achievement of separation from the mother or on the progress of individuation. Since masculinity is defined through separation while femininity is defined through attachment, male gender identity is threatened by intimacy while female gender identity is threatened by separation. Thus males tend to have difficulty with relationships, while females tend to have problems with individuation (p. 8).

Despite crucial differences in developmental experience, the replication strategies of self-propagation versus other-nurturance remain deeply rooted as the biological sources of gender differentiation. It is the female of all mammals, not the male, that becomes pregnant, is equipped with milk-producing glands to nourish the newborn, as well as invariably involved, with or without paternal assistance, in the care and protection of the infant. Although humans have been emanicipated in great measure from the influence exerted by hormonal mechanisms, there remain sufficient vestiges to incline the human female to act in a manner akin to her mammalian ancestors.

No less impressive among the biological underpinnings of the self/male-other/female antithesis are data strongly suggestive of gender differences in competition versus cooperation. In their masterly review, *The Psychology of Sex Differences*, Maccoby and Jacklin (1974) present convincing evidence, at least within Western cultures, that boys, on the average, are more venturesome and physically aggressive than girls, engage in more competitive play and are less concerned than girls with maintaining peaceable or equalitarian relationships.

Gender differences in sensitivity to external stimuli are evident from birth. Girl neonates have been found more reactive than boys to touch and taste (Garai and Scheinfeld, 1968), to sound and light (Korner, 1973), including the sounds of other newborns' crying (Sage and Hoffman, 1976). Newborn girls engage in more reflexive smiling than boys (Korner, 1969), a communicative pattern that remains a persistent female trait into maturity. Six-month-old girls are more responsive to faces than to geometrical forms (Lewis, 1969). And Hall's (1978) comprehensive review of studies investigating the attentiveness and accuracy with which the genders decode nonverbal cues from others (e.g., emotional states) led her to conclude that females were appreciably and consistently superior across the life span, a superiority that suggests that the talent is intrinsic as opposed to experientially acquired. Females across wide age spans establish and maintain eye contact more than do males; they also show a superior memory for faces (Haviland and Malatesta, 1981). Insofar as social communication skills are concerned, females again show greater competence across a broad range of verbal tasks. In addition to these indicators of interpersonal sensitivity and sociality, infant girls are perceived by their caretakers as "softer" and more manageable than are boys (Rubin, Provenzano and Luria, 1974). Along this line, Haviland and Malatesta (1981) provide evidence for the view that male infants are perceived as more "irritable," whereas females were judged more as "consolable."

In summarizing the accounts which highly successful and achieving women give of themselves, Gilligan writes (1982):

> . . . all of the women describe a relationship, depicting their identity *in* the connection of future mother, present wife, adopted child, or past lover . . . [they] do not mention their academic or professional distinction . . . . If anything, they regard their professional activities as jeopardizing their own sense of themselves.

> . . . identity is defined in a context of relationship and judged by a standard of responsibility and care (pp. 159–160).

By contrast, Gilligan's review of the descriptions which achieving men provide regarding themselves leads her to comment as follows (1982):

TABLE 1
Correspondence of Evolutionary Polarities and Psychological Constructs

Psychological Constructs \ Evolutionary Polarities	Pleasure-Pain	Passive-Active	Self-Other
Principles of Learning	Positive and Negative Reinforcers of Learning	Respondent versus Operant Modes of Behavior	Internal versus External Controls of Reinforcement
Psychoanalytic Concepts	Instinctual Aims of the Id	Reality Apparatuses of the Ego	Self-Structures versus Object Relations
Components of Emotion/ Motivation	Pleasant and Unpleasant Valences of Emotion	Low versus High Intensities of Activation	Competitive versus Cooperative Dispositions of Motivation
Neurobiological Substrates	Substrates of Mood	Substrates of Arousal	Substrates of Gender

Although the world of self that men describe at times includes "people" and "deep attachments," no particular person or relationship is mentioned . . . Replacing the women's verbs of attachment are adjectives of separation . . . the male "I" is defined in separation.

Instead of attachment, individual achievement rivets the male imagination.

Power and separation secure the man in an identity achieved through work, but they leave him at a distance from others (pp. 160–163).

Finally, as if further evidence need be garnered for the self/ male-other/female antithesis, we may wish to draw on the deeper archetypes that D. P. McAdams has explored. McAdams (1985), in his life-story model of identity, provides us with a "taxonomy of imagoes," a set of fascinating portrayals drawn from historical characters and Greek gods and goddesses. Animated by the "power motive," and adhering to the "ideology of justice," are male archetypes such as the "ruler," the "swift traveller," and the "warrior," respectively exemplied by Zeus, Hermes, and Ares. Oriented by the "intimacy motive," and following the "ideology of care," McAdams lists such imagoes as the "loyal friend," the "caregiver," and the "lover," respectively epitomized by Hera, Demeter, and Aphrodite.

What more could we ask than to have both biology and Greek mythology on the side of our gender-related evolutionary antithesis of "self" and "other."

A more formal summary of the concordance between evolutionary model polarities and modern psychological constructs is presented in Table 1.

CHAPTER FOUR

NOSOLOGY

Deriving a Classification for a Personological Science

I know that most men, including those at ease with problems of the greatest complexity, can seldom accept either the simplest and most obvious truth if it be such as would oblige them to admit the falsity of conclusions which they have delighted in explaining to colleagues, which they have proudly taught to others, and which they have woven, thread by thread, into the fabric of their lives (Tolstoy, 1903).

McAdams' historic scheme for identifying the "deeper" character of personologic imagoes is both scholarly and intriguing, but most nosologies, that is, clinical classification systems (Millon, 1987b), are based more on formal procedures of systematic observation, mathematic analysis, or theoretic deduction. However, humans did develop reliable and useful classifications long before the advent of modern scientific thought and method. Information, skill, and instrumentation were achieved without "science" and its symbolic abstractions and techniques of research. If useful classifications could be acquired by intelligent observation and common sense alone, what special values are derived by applying the complicated and rigorous procedures required in developing explicit criteria, categorical homogeneity, and diagnostic efficiency? Is rigor, clarity, precision, and experimentation more than a compulsive and picayunish concern for details, more than the pursuit for the honorific "science" title? Are the labors of precise differentiation or identifying optimal cutting scores worth the time and effort involved?

There is little question in this "age of science" that the answer would be yes. But why? What are the distinguishing virtues of precision in one's terminology, the specification of observable conceptual referents, the analysis of covariant attribute clusters? What sets these procedures apart from everyday methods of categorizing knowledge?

Because the number of ways to observe, describe, and organize the natural world is infinite, the terms and concepts created to represent these activities are often confusing and obscure. For example, different words are used to describe the same behavior, and the same word is used for different behaviors. Some terms are narrow in focus, others are broad, and some are difficult to define. Because of the diversity of events to which one can attend, or the lack of precision in the language we employ, different processes are confused and similar events get scattered hodgepodge across a scientific landscape; as a consequence, communication gets bogged down in terminological obscurities and semantic controversies.

Scientific progress requires the logical ordering of a systematic taxonomy. Chemistry was a jumble of laboratory "recipes" and unconnected facts until Mendeleev arranged the periodic table in the nineteenth century, and thereby organized the elements and their relationship in one stroke. What once was "natural history" changed into biology when Linnaeus named and classified almost every known species of plant and animal. Darwin's *Origin of Species* provided a basis for explaining the relationships ordered in Linnaeus's *Systema naturae*.

Diversity among chemicals and biologic species was always manifestly evident. In physics, however, the variety of subatomic particles proved to be a most unwelcome discovery. Efforts to classify particles was regarded at first to be a tedious and fruitless chore. A retrospective analysis, however, shows that early taxonomies were crucial to understanding the fundamental constituents of both matter and energy. Moreover, the development of an orderly schema for categorizing physical phenomena proved extremely useful in efforts to achieve their unification, that is to weave together the diverse forces and particles of nature into one seamless tapestry. Theories that seek a fully unified physical science today are closely articulated with the taxonomy of matter and force built in the 1960s.

A major goal of classifying the phenomena comprising a scientific subject is to avoid the morass of confusion that prevails in its early phases of development. Not all phenomena related to a subject need be attended to at once. Certain elements may be selected from the vast range of possibilities because they seem consistent with logical conjectures. To ensure a degree of reliability or consistency among those interested in a subject, its elements are defined as precisely as possible and classified according to what appears to be their core similarities and differences. In subjects such as psychopathology and personology, these classes or categories may be given specific labels to represent them. The steps of definition and classification are necessary for systematizing scientific observation and knowledge, but they are not sufficient.

How, then, have psychopathology and personologic classifications come into being?

For the most part, traditional nosologies were the product of a slowly evolving accretion of clinical experience, fostered and formalized periodically by the systematizing efforts of respected clinician-scholars such as Kraepelin (1899). One should expect empirical data or theoretical advances on matters of causality or structure to serve as the primary heuristic impetus, but such has not been the case. Psychiatric taxonomies have been formed by witnessing repetitive patterns of behavior and emotion among a small number of carefully studied mental patients. Etiologic hypotheses were subsequently generated to give meaning to these patterns of covariance (e. g., Hippocrates anchored differences in observed temperament to his humoral theory; Kraepelin distinguished two major categories of severe pathology, dementia praecox and manic-depressive disease, in terms of their ostensive divergent prognostic course). The elements comprising these theoretic notions were *post hoc*, however, imposed following the observation of data, rather than being a generative source. The most recent example of a clinically based classification, one tied explicitly to phenomenal observation and constructed by intention to be both atheoretic and nonquantitative, is, of course, the American Psychiatric Association's *Diagnostic and Statistical Manual of Mental Disorders*, the *DSM-III* (APA, 1980) and *DSM-III-R* (APA, 1987).

In large measure, clinically based nosologies gain their import and prominence by virtue of consensus and authority. Cumulative experience and habit are crystallized and subsequently confirmed by official bodies (Millon, 1987a). Specified criteria are denoted and articulated, acquiring definitional, if not stipulative powers, at least in the eyes of those who come to accept the criteria as infallible indicators.

Inasmuch as clinically based categories stem from the observations and inferences of diagnosticians, they comprise, in circular fashion, the very qualities that clinicians are most likely to see and deduce. Categories so constructed will not only direct future clinicians to focus on and to mirror these same observations, but may direct future nosologists away from potentially more useful signs with which to fathom less obvious patterns of clinical covariation. It is toward the end of penetrating beneath the sensory domain to more "latent" commonalities that classifiers turn either to numerical methods or to theoretical principles.

There has been a rapid proliferation of new and powerful mathematical techniques both for analyzing and synthesizing vast bodies of clinical data. This expansion has been accelerated by the ready availability of inexpensive computer hardware and software programs. Unfortunately, this mushrooming of new methodologies has progressed more rapidly than its fruits can be digested.

In his usual perspicacious manner, Kendell's comment on mathematic analyses (1975) is no less apt today as earlier:

> Looking back on the various studies published in the last twenty years it is clear that many investigators, clinicians, and statisticians, have had a naive, almost Baconian, attitude to the statistical techniques they were employing, putting in all the data at their disposal on the assumption that the computer would sort out the relevant from the irrelevant and expose the underlying principles and regularities, and assuming all that was required of them was to collect the data assiduously beforehand.
>
> Moreover, any statistician worth his salt is likely to be able, by judicious choice of patients and items, and of factoring or clustering procedures, to produce more or less what he wants to (p. 118).

Relationship Between Theory and Nosology

As knowledge advances, overt similarities, be they derived clinically or analyzed quantitatively, have been found to be an insufficient, if not false basis for cohering categories and imbuing them with scientific meaning (Smith and Medin, 1981). As the eminent philosophers of science, Hempel (1965) and Quine (1977), have pointed out, it is theory that provides the glue that holds a classification together and gives it both its scientific and clinical relevance. In his discussion of classificatory concepts, Hempel wrote (1965):

> . . . the development of a scientific discipline may often be said to proceed from an initial "natural history" stage . . . to subsequent more and more "theoretical" stages . . . The vocabulary required in the early stages of this development will be largely observational . . . The shift toward theoretical systematization is marked by the introduction of new, "theoretical" terms . . . more or less removed from the level of directly observable things and events . . . .
>
> These terms have a distinct meaning and function only in the context of a corresponding theory (pp. 139–140).

Quine makes a parallel case for the use of theories in determining category membership. Noting the usual progression from what he terms an innate, similarity-based conception of classification to a theoretically oriented one, he wrote (1977):

> . . . one's sense of similarity or one's system of kinds develops and changes . . . as one matures . . . And at length standards of similarity set in which are geared to theoretical science. This development is . . . away from the immediate, subjective, animal sense of similarity to

the remoter objectivity of a similarity determined by scientific hypotheses . . . and constructs. Things are similar in the later or theoretical sense to the degree that they are . . . revealed by science (p. 171).

What are the essential elements that distinguish between a true, theoretically deduced nosology and one that provides a mere explanatory summary of known observations and inferences?

Simply stated, the answer lies in its power to *generate* concepts, propositions, and categories other than those used to construct it. This generative power is what Hempel (1965) meant by the "systematic import" of a scientific classification. In contrasting what are familarly known as "natural" (theoretically guided, deductively based) and "artificial" (conceptually barren, similarity based) classifications, Hempel wrote (1965):

> Distinctions between "natural" and "artificial" classifications may well be explicated as referring to the difference between classifications that are scientifically fruitful and those that are not: in a classification of the former kind, those characteristics of the elements which serve as criteria of membership in a given class are associated, universally or with high probability, with more or less extensive clusters of other characteristics.

> Classification of this sort should be viewed as somehow having objective existence in nature, as "carving nature at the joints" in contradistinction of "artifical" classifications, in which the defining characteristics have few explanatory or predictive connections with other traits.

> In the course of scientific development, classifications defined by reference to manifest, observable characteristics will tend to give way to systems based on theoretical concepts (pp. 146–148).

What makes evolutionary theory as meritorious as proposed? Is the three-part polarity schema truly coextensive with the origins of the universe, the procession of organic life, as well as its modes of ecologic adaptation? Is it a mere conjectural fantasy? Or is there "justification" for pursuing it further?

Owing to the mathematical and deductive insights of our colleagues in physics, we have a deeper and clearer sense of the early evolution and structural relations among matter and energy. So too has knowledge progressed in our studies of physical chemistry, microbiology, evolutionary theory, population biology, ecology, and ethology. How odd it is (is it not?) that we have only now again begun to investigate—as we did at the turn of the last century—the interface between the basic building blocks of physical nature and the nature of life as we experience and live it personally? How much more is known today, yet how hesitant are people to undertake a serious rapprochement. As Barash has commented (1982):

> Like ships passing in the night, evolutionary biology and the social sciences have rarely even taken serious notice of each other, although admittedly, many introductory psychology texts give an obligatory toot of the Darwinian horn somewhere in the first chapter . . . before passing on to discuss human behavior as though it were determined only by environmental factors (p. 7).

Barash, a spokesperson for the sociobiologic perspective within psychology, dismisses the view that human behavior is rigidly programmed in our genes; on the other hand, he asserts that it is equally improbable that the two are "totally uncoupled." Commenting that serious efforts to undergird the behavioral sciences with the constructs and principles of evolutionary biology is as audacious as it is overdue, Barash notes (1982):

> . . . as with any modelling effort, we start with the simple, see how far it takes us, and then either compli-

cate or discard it as it gets tested against reality. The data available thus far are certainly suggestive and lead to the hope that more will shortly be forthcoming, so that tests and possible falsification can be carried out. In the meanwhile, as Darwin said when he first read Malthus, at last we have something to work with (p. 8)!

The evolutionary model that has been presented in earlier chapters, as well as its biosocial-learning forerunner (Millon, 1969, 1981, 1986a), has generated several new personality categories, several of which have found their way into the *DSM-III* and *DSM-III-R* (Kernberg, 1984). Drawing on the threefold polarity framework—pain-pleasure, active-passive, self-other—a series of ten personality "prototypes" and three severe variants were deduced, of which a few have proved to be "original" derivations in the sense that they had never been formulated as categories in prior psychiatric nosologies (e. g., portraying and coining the avoidant personality designation, Millon, 1969). Progressive research will determine if the network of concepts comprising this theory provides an optimal structure for a comprehensive nosology of personality pathology. At the very least, it contributes to the view that formal theory can lead to the deduction of new categories worthy of consensual verification.

Brief note should be made, before proceeding, to the utility of the evolutionary schema as a basis for characterizing so-called "normal" personality variants (Millon, in press). Normal individuals exhibit a reasonable balance between each of the polarity pairs. Not all individuals fall at the center, of course. Individual differences in both personality features and overall style will reflect the relative positions and strengths of each polarity component. A particularly "healthy" person, for example, would be one who is high on both self *and* other, indicating a solid sense of self-worth, combined with a genuine sensitivity to the needs of others.

Given its length, it would be only kind to refresh the reader's memory of the suggested four-part structure of a clinical science proposed in the first few pages of this book. In well-developed domains of clinical endeavor, a nosology, the second element of a clinical science, is derived logically from the major constructs and propositions of an undergirding *theory*, the first of the four constituents. In later sections we will briefly summarize the third and fourth ingredients, those composed of its underlying assessment *instruments* and its *interventions*, that is, its strategies and techniques of therapy.

Before proceeding to elaborate the theory-derived nosology of personality disorders, i. e., Axis II of the *DSM*, it should be recorded that the theory also provides a basis for deriving the so-called "clinical syndromes" that comprise Axis I. To illustrate briefly, the most prevalent mental disorder according to recent epidemiologic studies is that of the anxiety disorders. Without explicating its several variants, a low "pain" threshold on the pleasure-pain polarity would dispose such individuals to be sensitive to punishments which, depending on covariant polarity positions, might result in the acquisition of complex trait characteristics, such as ease of discouragement, low self-esteem, cautiousness, and social phobias. Similarly, a low "pleasure" threshold on the same polarity might make such individuals prone to experience joy and satisfaction with great ease; again, depending on covariant polarity positions, such persons might be inclined toward impulsiveness and hedonic pursuits, be intolerant of frustration and delay and, at the clinical level, give evidence of a susceptibility to manic episodes.

To use musical metaphors, *DSM-III's* Axis I clinical syndromes are "composed" essentially of a single theme or subject (e. g., anxiety, depression), a salient melodic line that may vary in its rhythm and harmony, changing little except in its timing, cadence, and progression. In contrast, the diversely expressed disorders that comprise Axis II seem constructed more in accord with the compositional structure known as the fugue where there is a dovetailing of two or more melodic lines. Framed in the sonata style, the opening exposition in the fugue begins when an introductory theme is announced (or analogously in psychopathology, a series of clinical symptoms become evident), following which a second and perhaps third, and essentially independent set of themes emerge in the form of "answers" to the first (akin to the unfolding expression of underlying personality traits). As the complexity of the fugue is revealed (we now have identified a full-blown personality disorder), variants of the introductory theme (that is, the initial symptom picture) develop "counter-subjects" (less observable, inferred traits) which are interwoven with the preceding in accord with well-known harmonic rules (comparably, mechanisms that regulate intrapsychic dynamics). This matrix of entwined melodic lines progresses over time in an episodic fashion, occasionally augmented, at other times diminished. It is sequenced to follow its evolving contrapuntal structure, unfolding a musical quilt, if you will, or better yet, an interlaced tapestry (the development and linkages of several psychological traits). To build this metaphorical elaboration further, not only may personality be viewed much like a fugue, but the melodic lines of its psychological counterpoints are comprised of the three evolutionary themes presented in preceding pages (the polarities, that is). Thus, some fugues are rhythmically vigorous and rousing (high "active"), others kindle a sweet sentimentality (high "other"), still others evoke a somber and anguished mood (high "pain"), and so on. When the counterpoint of the three polarities is harmonically balanced, we observe a well-functioning or so-called normal person; when deficiencies, imbalances, or conflicts exist among them, we observe one or another variant of the personality disorders.

Personalities we have termed *deficient* lack the capacity to experience or to enact certain aspects of the three polarities (e. g., the schizoid has a faulty substrate for both "pleasure" and "pain"); those spoken of as *imbalanced* lean strongly toward one or another extreme of a polarity (e. g., the dependent is oriented almost exclusively to receiving the support and nurturance of "others"); and those we judge in *conflict* struggle with ambivalences toward opposing ends of a bipolarity (e. g., the passive-aggressive vacillates between adhering to the expectancies of "others" versus enacting what is wished for one's "self").

A theory founded on the principles of more basic and established sciences should be more integrative and unifying than systems that are less consonant or firmly anchored. It should be able to derive, with a *single set* of constructs and propositions, *all* of the elements comprising its subject domain, in this case that of the personality disorders. As is *not* common in the personality domain, one set of concepts should suffice to "explain" narcissistic personalities, avoidant personalities, compulsive personalities, and so on. In this regard, the evolutionary model should match one of the great appeals of early psychoanalytic theory, in the latter case the derivation of *several* character types from a single developmental model of psychosexual stages.

In addition to the evolutionary theory's effort to provide explanatory hypotheses for the full range of personalities, it should be noted that its focus is on the *molar* level of personality disorders, rather than on the *molecular* level of symptoms and traits. It should be noted further that the theory was designed to be deductive rather than merely explanatory. That would have been the case had nothing been known concerning the features that characterize the personality disorders. That knowledge, of course, has been accessible for centuries, described brilliantly and analyzed incisively by observers in both ancient and modern times. Hence, much of what the evolutionary model provides is mere explanation, a way of explicating and interpreting the elements and processes of which these well-known character types are composed. On the other hand, in its earlier version (Millon, 1969), the theory was, in fact, generative in that it "filled some of the spaces" through deduction (e. g., both "avoidant" and "narcissistic" personality disorders were derived or brought into clearer light in this manner).

Applying the Polarity Model to the *DSM* Personality Disorders

Before detailing how the clinical features of the *DSM-III-R*, Axis II personality disorders can be coordinated to the evolutionary model, it will be useful to record a number of matters that should be considered when combining all three of the polarities. Elaborating what was stated or implied previously, personality, normal or disordered, is conceived as a complex of psychic structures and functions designed:

1. To enhance and to preserve life by maximizing "pleasure" and minimizing "pain." Pleasure and pain are *bipolar*, that is, separate dimensions; a person can be high or low on either or both, for example, schizoids experience little pleasure *and* little pain. Pleasure and pain are conceptual antitheses or opposites; each end has it own significance rather than exhibiting merely different levels or degrees of the same phenomenon, for example, pleasure is not a low (or high) level of pain, nor is pain a high (or low) level of pleasure.

2. To employ modes of behavior and thought that will maximize ecologic adaptation by achieving an optimal balance between "passive" accommodation and "active" modification. Passivity and activity represent a *unipolar* dimension, that is, they correspond essentially to quantitative differences in degree on a single continuum or gradient of motion or performance. In other words, a person cannot engage in both minimal passivity and minimal activity; the less they do of one, the more they do of the other.

3. To pursue strategies of behavior, emotion, and thought that maximize replicative success by achieving an optimal balance between "self" propagation and the nurturance of

"others." As with pleasure and pain, self and other are bipolar, comprising two independent and antithetical dimensions; persons may simultaneously be high or low on either or both. For example, avoidants typically express little interest nor gain much pleasure from either self or others; by contrast, to be focused on the welfare of others does not preclude self-interest.

It is not only the bipolarity structure and, hence, the greater number of variations that may arise in the pleasure-pain and self-other spheres that accounts for the observation that each gives rise to more and greater *sturm und drang* than is found in the passive-active polarity. That conflicts and reversals occur with greater frequency within the bipolarities is, in part, a simple arithmetic consequence, but no less contributory is the weighty psychic significance of the many and intense experiential variations of pleasure and pain, and of self and others.

It appears that dispositions toward one or another of the extremes of the three polarities are *not* entirely independent of one another. For example, an inclination toward experiencing psychic "pain" may be intrinsically related to the "other" oriented strategy; this hypothesis seems plausible given that the female gender is more other-oriented than the male and hence is more likely to be empathically sensitive to the discomforts of others and to needs of theirs that require care. Similarly, an "inherent" inclination to experience "pleasure" is more rather than less likely to *become* associated with the activity than the passivity mode, given the opportunity for each act to achieve a greater reward-per-unit of effort.

The preceding hypotheses that dispositions toward one polar extreme might increase the probability of possessing an extreme position on another does not argue for the view that there are many such covariances or that they claim particularly high probabilities when they occur. A quite wide range of polarity interrelationships are formed; only a limited number are likely to manifest themselves in pathologic polar extremes.

Three additional points may usefully be made to illustrate the combinatorial variations among the three polarities.

At the simplest level of analysis a number of personologic consequences of a single polar extreme will be examined. A high standing on the pain pole—a position typically associated with a disposition to experience anxiety—will be used for this purpose. The upshot of this singular sensitivity will take different forms depending on a variety of factors which lead to the learning of diverse styles of "anxiety-coping." For example, *avoidants* learn to deal with their pervasively experienced anxiety-sensitivity by removing themselves "across the board," that is, actively withdrawing from most relationships unless strong assurances of acceptance are given. The *compulsive*, often equally prone to experience anxiety, has learned that there are sanctioned but limited spheres of acceptable conduct; the compulsive reduces anxiety by restricting activities only to those which are permitted by more powerful and potentially rejecting others, as well as to adhere carefully to rules so that unacceptable boundaries will not be transgressed. And the anxiety-prone *paranoid* has learned to neutralize pain by constructing a semidelusional pseudocommunity (Cameron, 1963), one in which environmental realities are transformed to make them more tolerable and less threatening, albeit not very successfully. In sum, a high standing at the pain pole leads not to one, but to diverse personality outcomes.

Another of the polar extremes will be selected to illustrate the diversity of forms that coping styles may take as a function of covariant polarity positions; in this case reference will be made to a shared position on the "passivity" pole. Five primary Axis II disorders demonstrate the passive style, but their passivity derives from and is expressed in appreciably different ways that reflect disparate polarity combinations. *Schizoids*, for example, are passive owing to their relative incapacity to experience pleasure and pain; without the rewards these emotional valences normally activate, they will be devoid of the drive to acquire rewards, leading them to become rather indifferent and passive observers. *Dependents* typically are average on the pleasure and pain polarity, yet they are usually no less passive than schizoids. Strongly oriented to "others," they are notably weak with regard to "self." Passivity for them stems from deficits in self-confidence and competence, leading to deficits in initiative and autonomous skills, as well as a tendency to wait passively while others assume leadership and guide them. Passivity among *compulsives* stems from their fear of acting independently, owing to intrapsychic resolutions they have made to quell hidden thoughts and emotions generated by their intense self-other ambivalence. Dreading the possibility of making mistakes or engaging in disapproved behaviors, they became indecisive, immobilized, restrained, and passive. High on pain, and low on both pleasure and self, the *self-defeating* personality operates on the assumption that they dare not expect, nor do they deserve to have life go their way; giving up any efforts to achieve a life that accords with their "true" desires, they passively submit to others' wishes, acquiescently accepting their fate. Finally, *narcissists*, especially high on self and low on others, benignly assume that "good things" will come their way with little or no effort on their part; this passive exploitation of others is a consequence of the unexplored confidence that underlies their self-centered presumptions.

To turn to slightly more complex cases, there are individuals with appreciably different personality disorders who are often characterized by highly similar clinical features. To illustrate: To be correctly judged as "humorless and emotionally restricted" may be the result of diverse polarity combinations. *Schizoids*, as noted previously, are typically at the low end of both dimensions of the pleasure-pain bipolarity; experiencing little joy, sadness or anger, they are quite humorless and though not restricted emotionally, do lack emotional expressiveness and spontaneity. By contrast, *avoidants* are notably high at the pain polar extreme; whatever their other traits may be, they are disposed to chance neither interpersonal humor nor an emotional openness. Finally, the self-other conflicted *compulsive* has learned to deny "self" expression as a means of assuring the approval of others; rarely will the compulsive permit his or her guard down, lest any true "oppositional" feelings be betrayed; a compulsive rarely is relaxed sufficiently to engage in easy humor, nor willing to expose any contained emotions. All three personalities are humorless and emotionally restricted, but from rather different polarity combinations.

The seeming theoretic fertility of the polarities secures but a first step toward a systematic personality nosology. Convincing professionals of the validity of the schema requires detailed explications, on the one hand, and unequivocal evidence of utility, on the other. We must not only clarify what is meant by each term comprising the polarities—for example, identify or illustrate their empirical referents, but also specify ways in which they combine and manifest themselves clinically. It is toward those ends that the following paragraphs are addressed. Specifically, each of the *DSM-III-R*, Axis II disorders will be described and, in part, interpreted in terms of the polarity model.

1. *Schizoid Personality.* On what basis can pathology in the level or capacity of either the pain and pleasure polarities be seen as relevant to personality disorders? Several possibilities present themselves. Schizoid patients are those in which both polarity systems are *deficient*, that is, they lack the capacity, relatively speaking, to experience life's events either as painful or pleasurable. They tend to be apathetic, listless, distant, and asocial. Affectionate needs and emotional feelings are minimal and the individual functions as a passive observer detached from the rewards and affections as well as from the demands of human relationships. Schizoid patients characterized by a diminished capacity to experience *both* pleasure and pain seem neither interested in personal enjoyment or social satisfaction, nor do they evidence much discomfort with personal difficulties or social discord. Deficits such as these across the entire pleasure-pain polarity underlie what is termed the *passive-detached* style.

Aspects of the developmental background and clinical features of these personalities may provide the reader with a sense of how abstract concept such as pain and pleasure can be conceived as relevant etiologic attributes. Schizoid patients neither strive for rewards nor seek to avoid punishment (relatively speaking). Deficiencies such as these may arise from several etiologic sources. Some may lack the constitutional makeup requisite for seeking, sensing, or discriminating pleasurable or painful events. Others may have been deprived of the stimulus nourishment necessary for the maturation of motivational or emotional capacities. A third group may have been exposed to irrational and confusing family communications or to contradictory patterns of learning, both of which may result in cognitive perplexities or motivational apathies. Whatever the complex of causes may have been, schizoid patients acquire little or no body of either pleasurable or painful objects to motivate their behaviors.

2. *Avoidant Personalities.* The second clinically meaningful combination based on problems in the pleasure-pain polarity comprises patients with a diminished ability to experience pleasure, but with an unusual sensitivity and responsiveness to psychic pain. To them, life is vexatious, possessing few rewards and much anguish. This *imbalance* of heightened psychic pain and diminished psychic pleasure lies at the heart of the *DSM-III-R avoidant personality.* Both schizoids and avoidants share a minimal sense of joy and contentment; only one, the avoidant, is disposed also to feel sad or tormented. The theory groups these two personality, referring to them as *detached* patterns, the former, schizoid, noted as the passive-detached, the latter, avoidant, as the *active-detached.* Unable to experience pleasures either from self or others, both detached types tend to drift into isolating circumstances and self-alienated behaviors.

As noted, avoidants experience few pleasures in life, but do feel and react strongly to discomfort and punishment. It may be speculated that their neurological or physiochemical makeup may dispose them maximally to pain and minimally to pleasure; for example, centers of the limbic system may be unequally dense or may be disadvantageously wired to other brain regions. Equally possible, if not more probable, a history of harsh and rejecting early experiences may have oversensitized these individuals to psychic pain and anxiety. Exposed repeatedly to such events, avoidants may have learned not only to anticipate omnipresent threat, but to devise a widespread protective strategy of avoidance to minimize its recurrence. Experientially, avoidants often have been deprived of relationships that strengthen their feelings of competence and self-worth. Having a low self-opinion complicates matters further; they cannot turn to themselves as a worthy source of fantasized positive reinforcement. Ultimately, they learn to seek rewards neither from themselves nor from others. Many seem perpetually on guard, oriented solely to the avoidance of painful rejection and humiliation, ever-ready to distance themselves from an anxious anticipation of life's negatively reinforcing experiences. Reflecting fear and mistrust of others, they maintain a constant vigil lest their longing for affection result in a repetition of the pain they previously experienced with others. Despite desires to relate, they have learned that it is best to deny these feelings and maintain their interpersonal distance.

3. *Self-Defeating Personalities*.   Another disorder stems largely from a *reversal* of the pain-pleasure polarity. These patients interpret events and engage in relationships in a manner that is not only at variance with this deeply rooted polarity, but are contrary to the associations these life-promoting emotions usually acquire through learning. To the *self-defeating personality*, pain may be a preferred experience, passively accepted if not encouraged in intimate relationships. It is often intensified by purposeful self-denial and blame acceptance, may be aggravated by acts that engender difficulties, as well as by thoughts that exaggerate past misfortunes and anticipate future ones. Relating to others in an obsequious and self-sacrificing manner, these persons allow, if not encourage others to exploit or take advantage of them. Focusing on their very worst features, many assert that they deserve being shamed and humbled. To compound their pain and anguish, they actively and repetitively recall their past misfortunes, as well as transform otherwise fortunate circumstances into problematic outcomes. Typically acting in an unpresuming and self-effacing way, they often intensify their deficits and place themselves in an inferior light or abject position.

The background of the self-defeating personality has been a topic of considerable speculation for decades, most prominently in the psychoanalytic literature on masochism. This chapter is not the place to summarize this body of hypotheses. The role of biological anomalies in the inherent wiring of these personalities is a domain of speculation that cannot be totally dismissed, but it does stretch imagination beyond the usual range of plausibility. Not so incredulous are hypotheses of a social-learning or developmental nature. For example, by virtue of circumstantial association, elements normally evocative of pain and pleasure could very well become transposed or interconnected; thus, among future self-defeatists the pain of physical brutality or the anguish of verbal conflict may have been followed repetitively by love and intimacy, leading to the learned assumption that fractious provocations are a necessary precursor to ultimate acceptance and tenderness. In a more complicated sequence, guilt absolution may have been successfully achieved by repeated self-abasement, acts that generalize over time into a broad pattern of self-denial and servility that preventively "undoes" negative future consequences.

4. Sadistic Personalities. There are other patients in which the usual properties associated with pain and pleasure are conflicted or reversed. As with the self-defeating, these patients not only seek or create objectively "painful" events, but experience them as "pleasurable." This second variant of pain-pleasure reversal, what we term the *aggressive* personality (*DSM-III-R* sadistic), considers pain (stress, fear, cruelty) rather than pleasure to be the preferred mode of relating to others; in contrast to the self-defeating, this individual assumes an active role in controlling, dominating, and abusing others. Acts that humiliate, demean, if not brutalize, are experienced as pleasurable. We have grouped the self-defeating and aggressive personalities under the label "discordant patterns" to reflect, on the one hand, the dissonant structure of their pain-pleasure systems and, on the other, the conflictive character of their interpersonal relations. The self-defeating type, being on the receiving end of these fractious relationships, is referred to as the *passive-discordant*, whereas the latter, more expressive aggressive type, is termed the *active-discordant*.

The inclusion of the aggressive (or sadistic) personality style extends the boundaries of the *DSM-III-R* in a new and important direction, one that recognizes individuals who are not judged publicly to be antisocial, but whose actions signify personal pleasure and satisfaction in behaviors that humiliate others and violate their rights and feelings. Depending on social class and other moderating factors, they may parallel the clinical features of what is known in the literature as the sadistic character or, on the other hand, display character styles akin to the more competitive variant of the "Type A" personality. They are generally hostile, pervasively combative, and appear indifferent to, if not pleased, by the destructive consequences of their contentious, if not abusive and brutal behaviors. Although many cloak their more malicious and power-oriented tendencies in publicly approved roles and vocations, they give themselves away in their dominating, antagonistic, and frequent persecutory actions. As is all too well known, competitive ambition and social brutality may readily be reinforced as a means to security, status, and pleasure in our society by demonstrably resulting in personal achievement and dominance over others.

5. *Dependent Personalities.* Following the polarity model, one must ask whether particular clinical consequences occur among individuals who are markedly *imbalanced* by virtue of turning almost exclusively either toward *others* or toward them*selves* as a means of experiencing pleasure and avoiding pain. Such persons differ from the two detached and the two discordant types discussed previously; for example, neither detached type experiences pleasure from self or others. Personalities whose difficulties are traceable to the pathology of choosing one or the other polar end of the self-other dimension do experience both pain and pleasure, and do experience them in a consonant, nonreversed manner; their pathology arises from the fact that they are tied almost exclusively *either* to others or to themselves as the source of these experiences. The distinction between these two contrasting reproductive strategies underlies what is termed the "dependent" and "independent" personality orientations. In later paragraphs we will describe the ambivalent orientation, those who are in conflict between turning toward self (maximizing propagation) or toward others (maximizing nurturance) as their replication styles. For the present, however, those termed as the dependent types will be described clinically.

Those with a dependency pathology have learned that feeling good, secure, confident, and so on—that is, those feelings associated with pleasure or the avoidance of pain—is provided almost exclusively in their relationship with others. Behaviorally, these persons display a strong need for external support and attention; should they be deprived of affection and nurturance they will experience marked discomfort, if not sadness and anxiety. Any number of early experiences may set the stage for this dependency imbalance. In the dependent personality we often see individuals who have been exposed to an overprotective training regimen and who thereby fail to acquire competencies for autonomy and initiative; experiencing peer failures and low self-esteem leads them to forego attempts at self-assertion and self-gratification. They learn early that rewarding experiences are not readily achieved by themselves but are secured better by leaning on others. They learn not only to turn to others as their source of nurturance and security, but to wait *passively* for others to take the initiative in providing safety and sustenance. Clinically, most are characterized by a search for relationships in which others will reliably furnish affection, protection, and leadership. Lacking both initiative and autonomy, they assume a passive role in interpersonal relations, accepting what kindness and support they may find, and willingly submitting to the wishes of others in order to maintain nurturance and security.

6. Histrionic Personalities. Also turning to others as their primary strategy are a group of personalities that take an "active" dependency stance. They achieve their goal of maximizing protection, nurturance, and reproductive success by engaging busily in a series of manipulative, seductive, gregarious, and attention-getting maneuvers. It is this active dependency *imbalance* that characterizes the behavior of the *DSM-III-R* histrionic personality, according to the theory.

Although they turn toward others to no lesser extent than do passive-dependents, these individuals appear on the surface to be quite dissimilar from their passive counterparts; this difference in overt style owes to the active-dependent's facile and enterprising manipulation of events, which maximizes the receipt of attention and favors, as well as avoids social disinterest and disapproval. These patients often show an insatiable, if not indiscriminate search for stimulation and affection. Their clever and often artful social behaviors give the appearance of an inner confidence and independent self-assurance; beneath this guise, however, lies a fear of genuine autonomy and a need for repeated signs of acceptance and approval. Tribute and affection must constantly be replenished and is sought from every interpersonal source in most social contexts.

7. Narcissistic Personalities. Patients falling into the "independent" personality pattern also exhibit an *imbalance* in their replication strategy; in this case, however, there is a primary reliance on self rather than others. They have learned that reproductive success, as well as maximum pleasure and minimum pain is achieved by turning exclusively to themselves. The tendency to focus on self follows two major lines of development.

In the first, the narcissistic personality, it reflects the

acquisition of a self-image of superior worth, learned largely in response to admiring and doting parents. Providing self-rewards are highly gratifying if one values oneself or possesses either a "real" or inflated sense of self-worth. Displaying manifest confidence, arrogance, and an exploitive egocentricity in social contexts, this self-orientation is termed the *passive-independent* style in the theory, since the individual "already" has all that is important—him- or herself.

Narcissistic individuals are noted by their egotistic self-involvement, experiencing primary pleasure simply by passively being or attending to themselves. Early experience has taught them to overvalue their self-worth; this confidence and superiority, perhaps founded on false premises, may be unsustainable by real or mature achievements. Nevertheless, they blithely assume that others will recognize their specialness. Hence, they maintain an air of arrogant self-assurance and, without much thought or even conscious intent, benignly exploit others to their own advantage. Although the tributes of others are both welcome and encouraged, their air of snobbish and pretentious superiority requires little confirmation either through genuine accomplishment or social approval. Their sublime confidence that things will work out well provides them with little incentive to engage in the reciprocal give and take of social life.

8. *Antisocial Personalities.* Those whom we characterize as exhibiting the *active*-independent orientation resemble the outlook, temperament, and socially unacceptable behaviors of the *DSM-III-R* antisocial personality disorder. They act to counter the expectation of pain at the hand of others; this is done by actively engaging in duplicitous or illegal behaviors in which they seek to exploit others for self-gain. Skeptical regarding the motives of others, they desire autonomy, and wish revenge for what are felt as past injustices. Many are irresponsible and impulsive, actions they see as justified because they judge others to be unreliable and disloyal. Insensitivity and ruthlessness with others are the primary means they have learned to head off abuse and victimization.

In contrast to the narcissistic personality, this second pattern of self-orientation develops as a form of protection and counteraction. These types turn to themselves, first to avoid the depredation they anticipate and, second, to compensate by furnishing self-generated rewards in their stead. Learning that they cannot depend on others these patients counterbalance this loss not only by trusting themselves alone, but also by actively seeking retribution for what they see as past humiliations. Turning to self and seeking actively to gain strength, power, and revenge, they act irresponsibly, exploiting and usurping what others possess as sweet reprisal. Their security is never fully "assured," even when they have aggrandized themselves beyond their lesser origins.

9. *Passive-Aggressive Personalities.* In both dependent and independent orientations, patients demonstrate pathology in that the strategy of being oriented *either* toward others or toward themselves is unbalanced, grossly one-sided. An imbalance toward self or other is not the only pattern seen in this polarity. "Normal" individuals, of course, exhibit a comfortable intermediary position within the bipolarities of self and others. Certain pathological personalities, those whom we shall speak of as "ambivalent," also are oriented both toward self and others, but they are in intense *conflict* between one *or* the other. A number of these patients, those represented in the *DSM-III-R* passive-aggressive personality, vacillate between others and self, behaving obediently one time, and reacting defiantly the next. Feeling intensely, yet unable to restore their ambivalence, they weave an erratic course from voicing their self-depreciation and guilt for failing to meet the expectations of others, to expressing stubborn negativism and resistance over having submitted to the wishes of others rather than their own. Patients whose conflicts are overt, worn on their sleeves, so to speak, are characterized in the theory as *actively ambiva-*

lent, a richer and more varied lot than the *DSM*'s portrayal of the passive-aggressive.

The struggle between following the rewards offered by others as opposed to those desired by self represents a conflict similar to those of the *passive-ambivalent* (obsessive-compulsives); however, the conflicts of actively ambivalent personalities remain close to consciousness and intrude into everyday life. These patients get themselves into endless wrangles and disappointments as they fluctuate between deference and obedience one time, and defiance and aggressive negativism the next. Their behavior displays an erratic pattern of explosive anger or stubbornness intermingled with periods of guilt and shame.

10. *Obsessive-Compulsive Personalities.* The other major *conflicted* pattern, the *DSM-III-R* obsessive-compulsive personality disorder, displays a picture of distinct other-directedness, a consistency in social compliance and interpersonal respect; their histories usually indicate their having been subjected to constraint and discipline, but *only* when they transgressed parental strictures and expectations. Beneath the conforming other-oriented veneer they exhibit are intense desires to rebel and assert their own self-oriented feelings and impulses. They are trapped in an ambivalence; to avoid intimidation and punishment they have learned to deny the validity of their own wishes and emotions and, in their stead, have adopted as "true" the values and precepts set forth by others. The disparity they sense between their own urges and the behaviors they must display to avoid condemnation often lead to omnipresent physical tensions and rigid psychological controls.

Etiologically, obsessive-compulsives are likely to have been intimidated and coerced into accepting standards imposed on them by others. As noted, their prudent, controlled, and perfectionistic ways derive from a conflict between hostility toward others and a fear of social disapproval. They resolve this ambivalence not only by suppressing resentment, but by over-conforming and by placing high demands on both themselves and others. Their disciplined self-restraint serves to control intense, though hidden oppositional and self-centered feelings, resulting in their characteristic hesitation, doubt, passivity, and public compliance. Behind their front of propriety and restraint lurks intense angry feelings that occasionally break through their controls.

Severe Personality Disorders

Three additional pathological personality disorders in the *DSM-III-R* are formulated in the theory to represent severe dysfunctional levels. They differ from the first ten patterns by several criteria, notably deficits in social competence and frequent (but readily reversible) psychotic episodes. Moreover, they almost invariably coexist with and are more intense variants of the basic ten personality disorders discussed in the previous pages—for example, schizotypals tend to exhibit more problematic features also seen among schizoids and/or avoidants. Less integrated in terms of their personality organization and less effective in coping than their ten milder counterparts, they are especially vulnerable to decompensate when faced with the everyday strains of life.

A question that should be asked concerns the criteria employed for considering one personality as more severe than another. A full rationale will not be elaborated here (see Millon, 1981). Note that the approach taken was to group the 13 Axis II personalities in accord with their *ecologic adaptability*. Severity was gauged in great measure therefore by estimating the probability that a particular personality orientation would fit in one or another of the several, typical sociocultural niches available in contemporary Western society. In other words, we sought to assess the likelihood, in a culture such as ours, that the personality style would be able to maintain its structural coherence and would be able to function in a socially acceptable and personally rewarding manner.

All three of the severe disorders are adaptively problematic, difficult to relate to socially, and often isolated, hostile, or confused; hence, they are not likely to elicit the interpersonal support that could bolster their flagging defenses and orient them to a more effective and satisfying lifestyle. Moreover, a clear breakdown in the cohesion of personality organization is seen in the first two of these disorders; the converse is evident in the third, where there is an overly rigid and narrow focus to the personality structure. In the former pair, there has been a dissolution or diffusion of ego capacities; in the latter pattern, there is an inelasticity and constriction of personality, giving rise to a fragility and inadaptability of adaptive functions.

a. *Schizotypal Personalities.* This personality disorder represents a cognitively dysfunctional and maladaptively detached orientation in the polarity theory. Schizotypal personalities experience minimal pleasure, have difficulty consistently differentiating between self and other strategies, as well as active and passive modes of adaptation. Most prefer social isolation with minimal personal attachments and obligations. Inclined to be either autistic or confused cognitively, they think tangentially and often appear self-absorbed and ruminative. Behavioral eccentricities are notable, and the individual is often perceived by others as strange or different. Depending on whether their pattern is basically more active or more passive, there will be either an anxious wariness and hypersensitivity or an emotional flattening and deficiency of affect. Estranged from external support systems, they are likely to have few subliminatory channels and fewer still sources for emotional nurturance and cognitive stability, the lack of which disposes them to social regressions and autistic preoccupations.

b. *Borderline Personalities.* This personality disorder corresponds to the theory's emotionally dysfunctional and maladaptively ambivalent polarity orientation. Conflicts exist across the board, between pleasure and pain, active and passive, and self and other. They seem unable to take a consistent, neutral, or balanced position among these polar extremes, tending to fluctuate from one end to the other. Each of these persons experiences intense endogenous moods, with recurring periods of dejection and apathy, often interspersed with spells of anger, anxiety, or euphoria. Among the features that distinguish them from their less severe personality covariants is the dysregulation of their affects, seen most clearly in the instability and lability of their moods. Additionally, many express, if not enact, recurring self-mutilating and suicidal thoughts. Some appear overly preoccupied with securing affection. Many have difficulty maintaining a consistent sense of identity. Interpersonally, most display a cognitive-affective ambivalence, evident in simultaneous feelings of rage, love, and guilt toward others. These features represent a low level of structural cohesion in their psychic organization. For many there is a split within both their interpersonal and their intrapsychic orientations. Unable to build inner structural coherence, they are unable to maintain a nonconflictual direction in their personal relationships, or a consistency in their defensive operations. There are fundamental intrapsychic dissensions, core splits between taking an independent *or* taking a dependent stance, between acting out impulsively *or* withdrawing into passive disengagement, following the wishes of others *or* damning them and doing the opposite of what they wish. They repeatedly undo or reverse the actions they previously took, thereby embedding further the reality of being internally divided.

c. *Paranoid Personalities.* Here are seen a vigilant mistrust of others and an edgy defensiveness against anticipated criticism and deception. Driven by a high sensitivity to pain (rejection, humiliation) and oriented strongly to the self polarity, these patients exhibit a touchy irritability, a need to assert themselves, not necessarily in action, but in an inner world of self-determined beliefs and assumptions. They are "prepared" to provoke social conflicts and

TABLE 2
Polarity Model and Its Personality Disorder Derivatives

Polarity	Existential Aim — Pleasure-Pain		Replication Strategy — Self-Other		
	Life Enhancement	Life Preservation	Reproductive Propagation		Reproductive Nurturance
Pathology Deficiency, Imbalance or Conflict	Pleasure – Pain – +	Pleasure ↺ Pain	Self – Other +	Self + Other –	Self ↺ Other
Adaptation Mode — DSM-III-R Personality Disorders					
Passive: Accommodation	Schizoid	Self-Defeating	Dependent	Narcissistic	Compulsive
Active: Modification	Avoidant	Sadistic	Histrionic	Antisocial	Passive-Aggressive
Dysfunctional	Schizotypal	Borderline/ Paranoid	Borderline	Paranoid	Borderline/ Paranoid

fractious circumstances as a means of gratifying their confused mix of *pain*-sensitivity and *self*-assertion. The interplay of these polarities perpetuate their pathology; not only is it sustained, but it is increased as in a vicious circle. There is an ever-present abrasive irritability and a tendency to precipitate exasperation and anger in others. Expressed often is a fear of losing self-autonomy, leading the patient to vigorously resist external influence and control. Whereas borderline patterns are noted by the instability of their polarity positions, paranoids are distinctive by virtue of the immutability and inflexibility of their respective positions.

As can be seen from the foregoing, it was both feasible and productive to employ the key dimensions of the bipolar model to make the clinical features of the ten basic "styles" of personality functioning more explicit, from the actively pain-sensitive avoidant to the passively self-centered narcissist, from the actively other-oriented histrionic to the self-other conflicted passive-aggressive. The bias toward adaptive modes that is inherent in an evolutionary thesis does not facilitate distinctions among personality structures, such as characterize the severe disorders. However, it does enable the identification of alternate styles in which these more pathological syndromes are expressed—hence, the clinical presence of frequent mixtures such as histrionic borderlines, sadistic paranoids, avoidant schizotypals, and passive-aggressive borderlines. An overall picture of the relationship among the evolutionary bipolarities and their relationship to the personality disorders is presented in Table 2.

CHAPTER FIVE

INSTRUMENTATION

Assessment of Personality Polarities, Domains, and Disorders

*W*ho *could remain unmoved when Freud seemed suddenly to plunge towards the origins? Suddenly he stepped out of the conscious into the unconscious, out of everywhere into nowhere, like some supreme explorer. He walks straight through the wall of sleep, and we hear him rumbling in the cavern of dreams. The impenetrable is not impenetrable, unconsciousness is not nothingness.*
(Lawrence, 1921)

Not all patients with the same personality diagnosis should be viewed as possessing the same problem. Platitudinous though this statement may be, care must be taken not to force patients into the procrustean beds of our theoretical models and nosological entities. Whether or not they are derived from mathematical analyses, clinical observations, or a systematic theory, all taxonomies are essentially composed of prototypal classes. Clinical categories must be conceived as flexible and dimensionally quantitative, permitting the full and distinctive configuration of characteristics of patients to be displayed (Millon, 1987b). The multiaxial schema of *DSM-III* is a step in the right direction in that it encourages multidimensional considerations (Axes I, II, IV), as well as multidiagnoses that approximate the natural heterogeneity of patients, such as portrayed in personality profiles.

Moreover, patients' behaviors differ in their degree of endurance and pervasiveness. Each patient displays this durability and pervasiveness only in certain of his or her characteristics; that is, each possesses a limited number of attributes that are resistant to changing times and situational influences, whereas other attributes are readily modified. Furthermore, the features exhibiting this consistency and stability in one patient may not be the same features exhibited by others. These core qualities of persistence and extensiveness appear only in characteristics that have become crucial in maintaining the patient's polarity balance and functional style. To illustrate: The "interpersonal" attribute of significance for one patient is being totally other-oriented, never differing or having conflict (dependent); for another, it may be interpersonally critical to keep one's distance from people so as to avoid the pain of rejection or humiliation (avoidant); for a third, the influential interpersonal characteristic may be that of asserting one's will and inflicting pain on others (sadistic).

132

Each personality disorder comprises a small and distinct group of primary attributes that persist over time and exhibit a high degree of consistency across situations (Mischel, 1984). These enduring (stable) and pervasive (consistent) characteristics are what we search for when we "diagnose" personality. The multimodal therapist, Arnold Lazarus (1981) and I approach the assessment task from appreciably different perspectives, I from personality theory and diagnosis, he from an atheoretical eclectic therapy. Both his and my methods intersect in many ways, and their implications point to similar concerns regarding therapy interventions.

Personality disorders may be fruitfully evaluated with a variety of different theoretical orientations and clinical techniques. Three relatively new approaches and instruments which I and my colleagues have been developing these past several years add to this armamentarium of assessment tools. The newest approach is directed to the most fundamental level of analysis. It seeks to determine the balance and pattern the patient exhibits among the three *evolutionary polarities*—this is achieved in conjunction with a recently constructed self-report inventory, the *Millon Personality Type Questionnaire* (MPTQ) (Millon, in press, a) The second approach attempts to uncover the distinctive attributes that characterize a patient by systematically examining eight *clinical domains* in which pathologies are usually manifested or inferred; this is achieved in part by the use of clinician judgments recorded on a new checklist, the *Millon Personality Disorder Checklist* (MPDC) (Millon, Tringone, Green, Sandberg, et al., in press, c). The third, and more established approach, coordinates patients self-reports into a configuration or profile that seeks to mirror the patient's syndromal pattern, in this case his or her constellation of *personality disorders*; the *Millon Clinical Multiaxial Inventory (MCMI)-II* (Millon, 1987b) represents this latter methodology.

The logic and features of the MPTQ will be only briefly noted here since the constructs it attempts to represent have been extensively discussed in earlier chapters. In contrast to the MPDC and MCMI-II, the MPTQ is designed to assess *non-clinical personality styles*. Its primary scales are organized to obtain quantitative scores on each of the three polarity pairs, permitting independent assessments of self and other, and of pain and pleasure; there is a single score for the unidimensional active-passive scale. Separate calculations are made to gauge the presence and degree of conflict (self versus other) or reversal (pain-pleasure) between pairs of polarities. A set of secondary scales permit the development of a "normal personality type profile," akin to that achieved with clinically oriented inventories such as the MCMI-II and MMPI-2.

Let us turn from the polarity-related MPTQ to the conceptual basis for the *clinical domain*-oriented MPDC. These domains will be elaborated to illustrate their logic and general utility. In addition to expanding the "diagnostic criteria" for the personality disorders (Millon, 1986a, 1986b), this approach seeks to advance the development of *clinician judgments* as a mode of personality assessment. Specifically, they comprise descriptive attributes in various clinical domains (e.g., interpersonal conduct, cognitive style) within which the polarities may be expressed and with which all of the personality disorders may be systematically compared; see Table 3 for the domains chosen for inclusion.

Several criteria were used to select and develop the clinical domains that comprise this assessment schema: (a) that they be varied in the features they embody; that is, not be limited just to behaviors or cognitions, but to encompass a full range of clinically relevant characteristics; (b) that they parallel, if not correspond, to many of our profession's current therapeutic modalities (e. g., *self*-oriented analytic techniques; methods for altering dysfunctional *cognitions*; procedures for modifying *interpersonal* conduct); and (c) that they not only be coordinated to the official *DSM* schema of personality disorder prototypes, as well as to the guiding model of evolutionary polarities, but also that each disorder be characterized by a distinctive feature within each clinical domain.

TABLE 3
Clinical Domains

(F) Functional Domains   (S) Structural Domains
Behavioral Level
(F) Expressive Acts (F) Interpersonal Conduct
Phenomenological Level
(F) Cognitive Style (S) Object Representations (S) Self-Image
Intrapsychic Level
(F) Regulatory Mechanisms (S) Morphologic Organization
Biophysical Level
(S) Mood/Temperament

Many signs, symptoms, and characteristics of patients can usefully be categorized and dimensionalized for purposes of clinical analysis. As portrayed in Table 3, one basis for organizing diagnostic features would be to distinguish them in accord with the *data levels* they represent, (e. g., biophysical, intrapsychic, phenomenological, and behavioral). This differentiation reflects the four historic approaches that characterize the study of psychopathology, namely, the biological, the psychoanalytic, the cognitive, and the behavioral (Millon 1967). Another, and obviously useful, schema for evaluating personality characteristics is to group them in accord with whether the data obtained derive primarily from the patient as opposed to those observed or inferred by the clinician.

It is useful to organize the clinical domains in a manner similar to distinctions drawn in the biological realm, that is, dividing them into *structural* and *functional* attributes. The basic sciences of anatomy and physiology, respectively, investigate embedded and essentially permanent structures, which serve, for example, as substrates for mood and memory, and processes that underlie functions which regulate internal dynamics and external transactions.

Dividing the characteristics of the psychological world into structural and functional realms is by no means a novel notion. Psychoanalytic theory has dealt since its inception with topographic constructs such as conscious, preconscious, and unconscious, and later with structural concepts such as id, ego, and superego; likewise, a host of quasi-stationary functional processes, such as the so-called ego apparatuses, have been posited and studied (Gill, 1963; Rapaport, 1959).

There are several benefits to differentiating the more-or-less stable and organized clinical attributes (structures) from those that represent processing and modulating features (functions). For the present, it will suffice simply to define the terms "function" and "structure" as they apply to personologic matters; we may then proceed to identify the eight domains that are most relevant to personality diagnosis, point out the data level in which they are displayed most prominently, and briefly outline which of the evolutionary polarities they are likely to tap most clearly.

Functional characteristics represent dynamic processes that transpire within the intrapsychic world and between the individual's self and psychosocial environment. For definitional purposes, we might say that functional domains represent "expressive modes of regulatory action," that is, behaviors, social conduct, cognitive processes, and unconscious mechanisms which manage, adjust, transform, coordinate, balance, discharge, and control the give and take of inner and outer life.

Not only are there several realms of regulatory actions (e.g., interpersonal, cognitive, unconscious), but there are numerous variations in the way each of these functional modalities is manifested or expressed (e. g., interpersonally aloof, interpersonally submissive, interpersonally exploitive). Every individual employs every modality in a lifetime, but individuals differ with respect to the domains they enact most frequently, and even more so, diverge in which of the expressive variations of these functions they typically manifest. Particular domains and expressive variations characterize certain personalities best. As noted, dissimilar individuals differ in which modalities they express most often, but these differences are largely a matter of *quantitative frequency* (dimensionality) and not *qualitative distinctness*.

Four functional domains relevant to the personality disorders will be briefly described. There are 13 variations, one associated with each personality, as detailed in Tables 4 through 7 (Millon, 1986b).

Expressive Acts

These attributes relate to the observables seen at the "behavioral level" of data, and are usually recorded by noting what and how the patient acts. Through inference, observations of overt behavior enable us to deduce either what the patient unknowingly reveals about him or herself or, often conversely, what he or she wishes others to think or to know about him or her. The range and character of expressive actions are not only wide and diverse, but they convey both distinctive and worthwhile clinical information, from communicating a sense of personal incompetence to exhibiting general defensiveness to demonstrating a disciplined self-control, and so on. This domain of clinical data is likely to be especially productive in differentiating patients on the passive-active polarity.

Interpersonal Conduct

A patient's style of relating to others also is noted essentially at the "behavioral" date level, and may be captured in a number of ways, such as how his or her actions impact on others, intended or otherwise, the attitudes that underlie, prompt, and give shape to these actions, the methods by which he or she

TABLE 4
Expressive Act Domain

Personality	
Schizoid	Lethargic: appears to be in a state of fatigue, low energy and lack of vitality; is phlegmatic, sluggish, displaying deficits in activation, motoric expressiveness, and spontaneity.
Avoidant	Guarded: warily scans environment for potential threats; overreacts to innocuous events and anxiously judges them to signify personal ridicule and threat.
Dependent	Incompetent: ill-equipped to assume mature and independent roles; is docile and passive, lacking functional competencies, avoiding self-assertion and withdrawing from adult responsibilities.
Histrionic	Affected: is overreactive, stimulus-seeking, and intolerant of inactivity, resulting in impulsive, unreflected, and theatrical responsiveness; describes penchant for momentary excitements, fleeting adventures and short-sighted hedonism.
Narcissistic	Arrogant: flouts conventional rules of shared social living, viewing them as naive or inapplicable to self; reveals a careless disregard for personal integrity and an indifference to the rights of others.
Antisocial	Impulsive: is impetuous and irrepressible, acting hastily and spontaneously in a restless, spur-of-the-moment manner; is shortsighted, incautious and imprudent, failing to plan ahead or consider alternatives, no less heed consequences.
Sadistic	Fearless: is unflinching, recklessly daring, thick-skinned and seemingly undeterred by pain; is attracted to challenge, risk and harm, as well as undaunted by danger and punishment.

TABLE 4 *(cont.)*
Expressive Act Domain

Personality *(cont.)*	
Compulsive	Disciplined: maintains a regulated, repetitively structured and highly organized life pattern; is perfectionistic, insisting that subordinates adhere to personally established rules and methods.
Passive-Aggressive	Stubborn: resists fulfilling expectancies of others, frequently exhibiting procrastination, inefficiency and erratic, as well as other contrary and irksome behaviors; reveals gratification in demoralizing and undermining the pleasures and aspirations of others.
Self-Defeating	Abstinent: presents self as nonindulgent, frugal and chaste, refraining from exhibiting signs of pleasure or attractiveness; acts in an unpresuming and self-effacing manner, preferring to place self in an inferior light or abject position.
Schizotypal	Aberrant: exhibits socially gauche habits and peculiar mannerisms; is perceived by others as eccentric, disposed to behave in an unobtrusively odd, aloof, curious, or bizarre manner.
Borderline	Precipitate: displays a desultory energy level with sudden, unexpected and impulsive outbursts; abrupt, endogenous shifts in drive state and in inhibitory control, places activation equilibrium in constant jeopardy.
Paranoid	Defensive: is vigilantly alert to anticipate and ward off expected derogation and deception; is tenacious and firmly resistant to sources of external influence and control.

TABLE 5
Interpersonal Conduct Domain

Personality	
Schizoid	Aloof: seems indifferent and remote, rarely responsive to the actions or feelings of others, possessing minimal "human" interests; fades into the background, is unobtrusive, has few close relationships and prefers a peripheral role in social, work, and family settings.
Avoidant	Aversive: reports extensive history of social pan-anxiety and distrust; seeks acceptance, but maintains distance and privacy to avoid anticipated humiliation and derogation.
Dependent	Submissive: subordinates needs to stronger, nurturing figure, without whom feels anxiously helpless; is compliant, conciliatory, placating, and self-sacrificing.
Histrionic	Flirtatious: actively solicits praise and manipulates others to gain needed reassurance, attention, and approval; is demanding, self-dramatizing, vain, and seductively exhibitionistic.
Narcissistic	Exploitive: feels entitled, is unempathic and expects special favors without assuming reciprocal responsibilities; shamelessly takes others for granted and uses them to enhance self and indulge desires.
Antisocial	Irresponsible: is untrustworthy and unreliable, failing to meet or intentionally negating personal obligations of a marital, parental, employment, or financial nature; actively violates established social codes through duplicitous or illegal behaviors.
Sadistic	Cruel: reveals satisfaction in intimidating, coercing, and humiliating others; regularly expresses verbally abusive and derisive social commentary, as well as exhibiting vicious, if not physically brutal, behavior.

TABLE 5 *(cont.)*
Interpersonal Conduct Domain

Personality *(cont.)*	
Compulsive	Respectful: exhibits unusual adherence to social conventions and proprieties; prefers polite, formal, and correct personal relationships.
Passive-Aggressive	Contrary: assumes conflicting and changing roles in social relationships, particularly dependent acquiescence and assertive independence; is concurrently or sequentially obstructive and intolerant of others, expressing either negative or incompatible attitudes.
Self-Defeating	Deferential: relates to others in a self-sacrificing, servile, and obsequious manner, allowing, if not encouraging others to exploit or take advantage; is self-abasing and solicits condemnation by accepting undeserved blame and courting unjust criticism.
Schizotypal	Secretive: prefers privacy and isolation, with few, highly tentative attachments and personal obligations; has drifted over time into increasingly peripheral vocational roles and clandestine social activities.
Borderline	Paradoxical: although needing attention and affection, is unpredictably contrary, manipulative and volatile, frequently eliciting rejection rather than support; reacts to fears of separation and isolation in angry, mercurial, and often self-damaging ways.
Paranoid	Provocative: displays a quarrelsome, fractious and abrasive attitude; precipitates exasperation and anger by a testing of loyalties and a searching preoccupation with hidden motives.

TABLE 6
Cognitive Style Domain

Personality	
Schizoid	Impoverished: seems deficient across broad spheres of knowledge and evidences vague and obscure thought processes that are below intellectual level; communication is easily derailed, loses its sequence of thought or is conveyed via a circuitous logic.
Avoidant	Distracted: is preoccupied and bothered by disruptive and often perplexing inner thoughts; the upsurge from within of irrelevant and digressive ideation upsets thought continuity and interferes with social communications.
Dependent	Naive: is easily persuaded, unsuspicious, and gullible; reveals a Pollyanna attitude toward interpersonal difficulties, watering down objective problems, and smoothing over troubling events.
Histrionic	Flighty: avoids introspective thought and is overly attentive to superficial and fleeting external events; integrates experiences poorly, resulting in scattered learning and thoughtless judgments.
Narcissistic	Expansive: has an undisciplined imagination and exhibits a preoccupation with immature fantasies of success, beauty, or love; is minimally constrained by objective reality. takes liberties with facts and often lies to redeem self-illusions.
Antisocial	Deviant: construes events and relationships in accord with socially unorthodox beliefs and morals; is disdainful of traditional ideals and contemptuous of conventional rules.
Sadistic	Dogmatic: is strongly opinionated and close-minded, as well as unbending and obstinate in holding to one's preconceptions; exhibits a broad-ranging authoritariansim, social intolerance, and prejudice.

TABLE 6 *(cont.)*
Cognitive Style Domain

Personality *(cont.)*	
Compulsive	Constricted: constructs world in terms of rules, regulations, schedules and hierarchies; is unimaginative, indecisive, and notably upset by unfamiliar or novel ideas and customs.
Passive-Aggressive	Negativistic: is cynical, skeptical, and untrusting, approaching positive events with disbelief, and future possibilities with trepidation; has a misanthropic view of life, expressing disdain and caustic comments toward those experiencing good fortune.
Self-Defeating	Inconsistent: thinks and repeatedly expresses attitudes contrary to inner feelings; experiences contrasting emotions and conflicting thoughts toward self and others notably love, rage, and guilt.
Schizotypal	Autistic: mixes social communication with personal irrelevancies, circumstantial speech, ideas of reference, and metaphorical asides; is ruminative, appears self-absorbed and lost in daydreams with occasional magical thinking, obscure suspicions and a blurring of fantasy and reality.
Borderline	Capricious: experiences rapidly changing, fluctuating and antithetical perceptions or thoughts concerning passing events; vacillating and contradictory reactions are evoked in others by virtue of one's behaviors, creating, in turn, conflicting and confusing social feedback.
Paranoid	Suspicious: is skeptical, cynical, and mistrustful of the motives of others, construing innocuous events as signifying hidden or conspiratorial intent; reveals tendency to magnify tangential or minor social difficulties into proofs of duplicity, malice, and treachery.

TABLE 7
Regulatory Mechanism Domain

Personality	
Schizoid	Intellectualization: describes interpersonal and affective experiences in a matter of fact, abstract, impersonal, or mechanical manner; pays primary attention to formal and objective aspects of social and emotional events.
Avoidant	Fantasy: depends excessively on imagination to achieve need gratification and conflict resolution; withdraws into reveries as a means of safely discharging affectionate, as well as aggressive impulses.
Dependent	Introjection: is firmly devoted to another to strengthen the belief that an inseparable bond exists between them; jettisons any independent views in favor of those of another to preclude conflicts and threats to the relationship.
Histrionic	Dissociation: regularly alters self-presentations to create a succession of socially attractive but changing facades; engages in self-distracting activities to avoid reflecting on and integrating unpleasant thoughts and emotions.
Narcissistic	Rationalization: is self-deceptive and facile in devising plausible reasons to justify self-centered and socially inconsiderate behaviors; offers alibis to place oneself in the best possible light, despite evident shortcomings or failures.
Antisocial	Acting Out: inner tensions that might accrue by postponing the expression of offensive thoughts and malevolent actions are rarely constrained; socially repugnant impulses are not refashioned in sublimated forms, but are discharged directly in precipitous ways, usually without guilt.
Sadistic	Isolation: can be coldblooded and remarkably detached from an awareness of the impact of one's destructive acts; views objects of violation impersonally, as symbols of devalued groups devoid of human sensibilities.

TABLE 7 *(cont.)*
Regulatory Mechanism Domain

Personality *(cont.)*	
Compulsive	Reaction Formation: repeatedly presents positive thoughts and socially commendable behaviors that are diametrically opposite ones deeper, contrary and forbidden feelings; displays reasonableness and maturity when faced with circumstances that evoke anger or dismay in others.
Passive-Aggressive	Displacement: discharges anger and other troublesome emotions either indirectly or by shifting them from their instigator to settings or persons of lesser significance; expresses resentments by substitute or passive means, such as acting inept or perplexed, or behaving in a forgetful or indolent manner.
Self-Defeating	Devaluation; repetitively recalls past injustices and anticipates future disappointments as a means of raising distress to homeostatic levels; misconstrues, if not sabotages good fortune so as to enhance or maintain preferred suffering and pain.
Schizotypal	Undoing: bizarre mannerisms and idiosyncratic thoughts appear to reflect a retraction or reversal of previous acts or ideas that have stirred feelings of anxiety, conflict or guilt; ritualistic or "magical" behaviors serve to repent for or nullify assumed misdeeds or "evil" thoughts.
Borderline	Regression: retreats under stress to developmentally earlier levels of anxiety tolerance, impulse control, and social adaptation; among adolescents, is unable to cope with adult demands and conflicts, as evident in immature, if not increasingly infantile behaviors.
Paranoid	Projection: actively disowns undesirable personal traits and motives, and attributes them to others; remains blind to ones own unattractive behaviors and characteristics, yet is overalert to, and hypercritical of, similar features in others.

engages others to meet his or her needs, or his or her way of coping with social tensions and conflicts. Extrapolating from these observations, the clinician may construct an image of how the patient functions in relation to others, be it antagonistically, respectfully, aversively, secretively, and so on. Among the most fruitful attributes, interpersonal conduct may provide useful data on all three polarities, but especially that of self-other.

Cognitive Style

How the patient perceives events, focuses attention, processes information, organizes thoughts, and communicates reactions and ideas to others represent data at the "phenomenological" level, and are among the most useful indices to the clinician of the patient's distinctive way of functioning. By synthesizing these signs and symptoms, it may be possible to identify indications of what may be termed an impoverished style, or distracted thinking, or cognitive flightiness, or constricted thought, and so on. As with interpersonal conduct, cognitive style may be productive in uncovering data on all three polarities; the passive-active dimension may be especially well identified by analyses of this attribute.

Regulatory Mechanism

Although "mechanisms" of self-protection, need gratification, and conflict resolution are consciously recognized at times, they represent data derived primarily at the "intrapsychic" level, and thereby avoid reflective appraisal. As such, they often begin a sequence of events that intensifies the very problems they were intended to circumvent. Mechanisms usually represent internal processes and, hence, are more difficult to discern and describe than processes anchored closer to the observable world. Despite the methodological problems they present, the task of identifying which mechanisms are chosen (e. g., rationalization, displacement, reaction formation) and the extent to which they are employed is extremely useful in a comprehensive personality assessment. Inferences pertaining to this attribute are likely to be effective in yielding distinctions along both the passive-active and pleasure-pain polarities.

Structural attributes represent a deeply embedded and relatively enduring template of imprinted memories, attitudes, needs, fears, conflicts, and so on, which guide the experience and transform the nature of ongoing life events. Psychic structures have an orienting and preemptive effect in that they alter the character of action and the impact of subsequent experiences in line with preformed inclinations and expectancies. By selectively lowering thresholds for transactions that are consonant with either constitutional proclivities or early learnings, future events are often experienced as variations of the past. The following describes both the character and persistence of these structural residues of early experience (Millon, 1969).

Significant experiences of early life many never recur again, but their effects remain and leave their mark. Physiologically, we may say they have etched a neurochemical change; psychologically, they are registered as memories, a permanent trace and an embedded internal stimulus. In contrast to the fleeting stimuli of the external world, these memory traces become part and parcel of every stimulus complex which activates behavior. Once registered, the effects of the past are indelible, incessant, and inescapable. They now are intrinsic elements of the individual's makeup; they latch on and intrude into the current events of life, coloring, transforming and distorting the passing scene. Although the residuals of subsequent experiences may override them, becoming more dominant internal stimuli, the presence of earlier memory traces remains in one form or another. In every thought and action, the individual cannot help but carry these remnants into the present. Every current behavior is a perpetuation, then, of the past, a continuation and intrusion of these inner stimulus traces.

The residuals of the past do more than passively contribute their share to the present. By temporal precedence, if nothing else, they guide, shape or distort the character of current events. Not only are they ever present, then, but they operate insidiously to transform new stimulus experiences in line with the past (p. 200).

For purposes of definition, structural domains may be conceived as "substrates and action dispositions of a quasi-permanent nature." Possessing a network of interconnecting pathways, these structures contain the internalized residues of the past in the form of memories and affects that are associated intrapsychically with conceptions of self and others.

Four structural domains relevant to personality will be briefly described. There are 13 variations, one for each personality prototype, as presented in Tables 8 through 11 (Millon, 1986b).

Self-Image

As the inner world of symbols is mastered through development, the "swirl" of events that buffet the young child gives way to a growing sense of order and continuity. One major configuration emerges to impose a measure of sameness on an otherwise fluid environment, the perception of self-as-object, a distinct, ever-present, and identifiable "I" or "me." Self-identity stems largely from conceptions drawn at the "phenomenological" level of analysis. It is especially significant in that it provides a stable anchor to serve as a guidepost and to give continuity to changing experience. Most persons have an implicit sense of who they are, but differ greatly in the clarity and accuracy of their self-introspections. Few can articulate the psychic elements that comprise this image, such as stating knowingly whether they view themselves as primarily alienated, or inept, or complacent, or conscientious, and so on. As should be evident, this attribute is closely oriented to provide data on the "self" pole of the self-other polarity; also likely to be clarified are features relevant to the pleasure-pain polarity.

Object Representations

As noted previously, significant experiences from the past leave an inner imprint, a structural residue composed of memories, attitudes, and affects that serve as a substrate of dispositions for perceiving and reacting to life's ongoing events. As such, these representations inhere within the "phenomenological" realm. Analogous to the various organ systems of which the body is composed, both the character and substance of these internalized representations of significant figures and relationships of the past can be differentiated and analyzed for clinical purposes. Variations in the nature and content of this inner world can be associated with one or another personality and lead us to employ descriptive terms to represent them, such as shallow, vexatious, undifferentiated, concealed, and irreconcilable. Balancing the preceding attribute on "self," the focus of this attribute is clearly oriented to provide information on the "other" pole; the pleasure-pain aspects of other also should be usefully generated.

Morphologic Organization

The overall architecture that serves as a framework for an individual's psychic interior may display weakness in its structural cohesion, exhibit deficient coordination among its components, and possess few mechanisms to maintain balance and harmony, regulate internal conflicts, or mediate external pressures. The concept of morphologic organization refers to the structural strength, interior congruity, and functional efficacy of the personality system. "Organization" of the mind is almost exclusively derived from inferences at the "intrapsychic level" of analysis. It is a concept akin to and employed in conjunction with current psychoanalytic notions such as

TABLE 8
Self-Image Domain

Personality	
Schizoid	Complacent: reveals minimal introspection and awareness of self; seems impervious to the emotional and personal implications of everyday social life.
Avoidant	Alienated: sees self as a person who is socially isolated and rejected by others; devalues self-achievements and reports feelings of aloneness and emptiness, if not depersonalization.
Dependent	Inept: views self as weak, fragile, and inadequate; exhibits lack of self-confidence by belittling own aptitudes and competencies.
Histrionic	Sociable: views self as gregarious, stimulating, and charming; enjoys the image of attracting acquaintances and pursuing a busy and pleasure-oriented social life.
Narcissistic	Admirable: confidently exhibits self, acting in a self-assured manner and displaying achievements; has a sense of high self-worth, despite being seen by others as egotistic, inconsiderate, and arrogant.
Antisocial	Autonomous: sees self as unfettered by the restrictions of social customs and the restraints of personal loyalties; values the image and enjoys the sense of being free, unencumbered, and unconfined by persons, places, obligations, or routines.
Sadistic	Competitive: is proud to characterize self as assertively independent, vigorously energetic and realistically hardheaded; values aspects of self that present tough, domineering, and power-oriented image.

TABLE 8 *(cont.)*
Self-Image Domain

Personality *(cont.)*	
Compulsive	Conscientious: sees self as industrious, reliable, meticulous, and efficient; fearful of error or misjudgment and, hence overvalues aspects of self that exhibit discipline, perfection, prudence, and loyalty.
Passive-Aggressive	Discontented: sees self as misunderstood, unappreciated, and demeaned by others; recognizes being characteristically resentful, disgruntled, and disillusioned with life.
Self-Defeating	Undeserving: focuses on the very worst features of self, asserting thereby that one is worthy of being shamed, humbled, and debased; feels that one has failed to live up to the expectations of others and, hence, deserves to suffer painful consequences.
Schizotypal	Estranged: possesses permeable ego-boundaries, exhibiting recurrent social perplexities and illusions as well as experiences of depersonalization, derealization, and dissociation; sees self as forlorn, with repetitive thoughts of life's emptiness and meaninglessness.
Borderline	Uncertain: experiences the confusions of an immature, nebulous or wavering sense of identity; seeks to redeem precipitate actions and changing self-presentations with expressions of contrition and self-punitive behaviors.
Paranoid	Inviolable: has persistent ideas of self-importance and self-reference, asserting as personally derogatory and scurrilous, if not libelous, entirely innocuous actions and events; is pridefully independent and highly insular, experiencing intense fears, however, of losing identity, status, and powers of self-determination.

TABLE 9
Object Representations Domain

Personality	
Schizoid	Undifferentiated: inner representations are few in number and minimally articulated, largely devoid of the manifold percepts and memories, nor the dynamic interplay among drives and conflicts that typify even well-adjusted persons.
Avoidant	Vexatious: inner representations are composed of readily reactivated intense, and conflict-ridden memories, limited avenues of gratification, and few mechanisms to channel needs, bind impulses, resolve conflicts, or deflect external stressors.
Dependent	Immature: inner representations are composed of unsophisticated ideas and incomplete memories, rudimentary drives, and childlike impulses, as well as minimal competencies to manage and resolve stressors.
Histrionic	Shallow: inner representations are composed largely of superficial and segregated affects, memories, and conflicts, as well as facile drives and insubstantial mechanisms.
Narcissistic	Contrived: inner representations are composed far more than usual of illusory ideas and memories, synthetic drives and conflicts, and pretentious, if not simulated, percepts and attitudes, all of which are readily refashioned as the need arises.
Antisocial	Rebellious: inner representations comprise an ungovernable mix of revengeful attitudes and restive impulses driven to subvert established cultural ideals and mores, as well as to debase personal sentiments and material attainments of society which were denied them.
Sadistic	Pernicious: inner representations are best distinguished by the presence of strongly driven aggressive energies and malicious attitudes, as well as by a contrasting paucity of sentimental memories, tender affects, internal conflicts, shame, or guilt feelings.

TABLE 9 *(cont.)*
Object Representations Domain

Personality *(cont.)*	
Compulsive	Concealed: only those inner affects, attitudes, and actions which are socially approved are allowed conscious awareness or behavioral expression, resulting in gratification being highly regulated, forbidden impulses sequestered and tightly bound, personal and social conflicts defensively denied, kept from awareness, and all maintained under stringent control.
Passive-Aggressive	Oppositional: inner representations comprise a complex of countervailing inclinations and incompatible memories that are driven pervasively by strong dissident impulses designed to nullify the achievements and pleasures of others.
Self-Defeating	Debased: inner representations are composed of disparaged past memories and discredited achievements, of positive feelings and erotic drives transposed into their least attractive opposites, of internal conflicts intentionally aggravated, of mechanisms of anxiety reduction subverted by processes which intensify discomfort.
Schizotypal	Chaotic: inner representations consist of a jumble of piecemeal memories and percepts, random drives and impulses, and uncoordinated channels of regulation that are only fitfully competent for binding tensions, accommodating needs, and mediating conflicts.
Borderline	Incompatible: rudimentary and expediently devised, but repetitively aborted, learnings have led to perplexing memories, enigmatic attitudes, contradictory needs, antithetical emotions, erratic impulses, and opposing strategies for conflict reduction.
Paranoid	Unalterable: inner representations are precisely arranged in an unusual configuration of deeply held attitudes, unyielding percepts and implacable drives which, in turn, are aligned in an idiosyncratic and fixed hierarchy of tenacious memories, immutable cognitions, and irrevocable beliefs.

TABLE 10
Morphologic Organization Domain

Personality	
Schizoid	Meager: given an inner barrenness, a feeble drive to fulfill needs, and minimal pressures to defend against or resolve internal conflicts, nor to cope with external demands, internal structures may best be characterized by their limited coordination and sterile order.
Avoidant	Fragile: a precarious complex of tortuous emotions depend almost exclusively on a single modality for its resolution and discharge, that of avoidance, escape, and fantasy and, hence, when faced with unanticipated stress, there are few resources available to deploy and few positions to revert to, short of a regressive decompensation.
Dependent	Inchoate: owing to entrusting others with the responsibility to fulfill needs and to cope with adult tasks, there is both a deficit and a lack of diversity in internal mechanisms and regulatory controls, leaving a miscellany of relatively undeveloped and undifferentiated adaptive abilities, as well as an elementary system for functioning independently.
Histrionic	Disjoined: there exists a loosely knit and carelessly united conglomerate in which processes of internal regulation and control are scattered and unintegrated, with few methods for restraining impulses, coordinating defenses, and resolving conflicts, leading to mechanisms that must of necessity, be broad and sweeping to maintain psychic cohesion and stability, and, when successful, only further isolate and disconnect thoughts, feelings and actions.
Narcissistic	Spurious: coping and defensive strategies tend to be flimsy and transparent, appear more substantial and dynamically orchestrated than they are, regulating impulses only marginally, channeling needs with minimal restraint, and creating an inner world in which conflicts are dismissed, failures are quickly redeemed, and self-pride is effortlessly reasserted.

TABLE 10 *(cont.)*
Morphologic Organization Domain

Personality *(cont.)*	
Antisocial	Unbounded: inner defensive operations are noted by their paucity, as are efforts to curb refractory drives and attitudes, leading to easily transgressed controls, low thresholds for impulse discharge, few subliminatory channels, unfettered self-expression, and a marked intolerance of delay or frustration.
Sadistic	Eruptive: despite a generally cohesive structure composed of routinely adequate modulating controls, defenses, and expressive channels, surging, powerful and explosive energies of an aggressive and sexual nature produce precipitous outbursts that periodically overwhelm and overrun otherwise competent restraints.
Compulsive	Compartmentalized: psychic structures are rigidly organized in a tightly consolidated system that is clearly partitioned into numerous, distinct and segregated constellations of drive, memory, and cognition, with few open channels to permit interplay among these components.
Passive-Aggressive	Divergent: there is a clear division in the pattern of internal elements such that coping and defensive maneuvers are often directed toward incompatible goals, leaving major conflicts unresolved and psychic cohesion impossible by virtue of the fact that fulfillment of one drive or need inevitably nullifies or reverses another.
Self-Defeating	Inverted: owing to a significant reversal of the pain-pleasure polarity, structures have a dual quality—one more-or-less conventional, the other its obverse—resulting in a repetitive undoing of affect and intention, of a transposing of channels of need gratification with those leading to frustration, and of engaging in actions which produce antithetical, if not self-sabotaging, consequences.

TABLE 10 *(cont.)*
Morphologic Organization Domain

Personality *(cont.)*	
Schizotypal	Fragmented: coping and defensive operations are haphazardly ordered in a loose assemblage, leading to spasmodic and desultory actions in which primitive thoughts and affects are discharged directly, with few reality-based sublimations, and significant further disintegrations of structure likely under even modest stress.
Borderline	Diffused: inner structures exist in a dedifferentiated configuration in which a marked lack of clarity and distinctness is seen among elements, levels of consciousness occasionally blur and an easy flow occurs across boundaries that usually separate unrelated percepts, memories, and affects, all of which results in periodic dissolutions of what limited psychic order and cohesion is normally present.
Paranoid	Inelastic: systemic constriction and inflexibility of coping and defensive methods, as well as rigidly fixed channels of conflict mediation and need gratification, creates an overstrung and taut frame that is so uncompromising in its accommodation to changing circumstances that unanticipated stressors are likely to precipitate either explosive outbursts or inner shatterings.

borderline and psychotic levels, but this usage tends to be limited, relating essentially to quantitative degrees of integrative pathology, not to variations either in integrative character or configuration. "Stylistic" variants of this structural attribute may be employed to characterize each of the 13 personality prototypes; their distinctive organizational qualities are represented with descriptors such an inchoate, disjoined, and compartmentalized. Although impossible to observe directly and difficult to infer, nevertheless this important clinical attribute relates most directly to the structural character of "self" in the self-other polarity.

Mood/Temperament

Few observables are clinically more relevant from the "biophysical" level of data analysis than the predominant character of an individual's affect and the intensity and frequency with which he or she expresses it. The "meaning" of extreme emotions is easy to decode. This is not so with the more subtle moods and feelings that insidiously and repetitively pervade the patient's ongoing relationships and experiences. Not only are the expressive features of mood and drive conveyed by terms such as distraught, labile, fickle, or hostile communicated via self-report, but they are revealed as well, albeit indirectly, in the patient's level of activity, speech quality, and physical appearance. Clearly, the most useful aspect of this attribute as it relates to the theory is its utility in appraising features relevant to the pleasure-pain and active-passive polarities.

To summarize, the MPDC offers an opportunity for diagnosticians to systematically assess patients across a wide range of clinical domains. Cumulative ratings obtained with its recently published MPDC-III-R Form (Millon et al., in press, c) should enable clinicians to make diagnostic assignments in accord with the *DSM-III-R*, Axis II classification system. However, owing to the noninferential character of the *DSM's* criteria, this form of the MPDC encompasses only the domains of

TABLE 11
Mood/Temperament Domain

Personality	
Schizoid	Flat: is emotionally impassive, exhibiting an intrinsic unfeeling, cold and stark quality; reports weak affectionate or erotic needs, rarely displaying warm or intense feelings, and apparently unable to experience either pleasure, sadness, or anger in any depth.
Avoidant	Anguished: describes constant and confusing undercurrents of tension, sadness, and anger; vacillates between desire for affection, fear of rebuff, and numbness of feeling.
Dependent	Pacific: is characteristically warm, tender, and noncompetitive; timidly avoids social tension and interpersonal conflicts.
Histrionic	Fickle: displays short-lived dramatic and superficial emotions; is overreactive, impetuous, and exhibits tendencies to be easily enthused and as easily angered or bored.
Narcissistic	Insouciant: manifests a general air of nonchalance and imperturbability; appears cooly unimpressionable or buoyantly optimistic, except when narcissistic confidence is shaken, at which time either rage, shame, or emptiness is briefly displayed.
Antisocial	Callous: is insensitive, unempathetic, and cold-blooded, as expressed in a wide-ranging deficit in social charitableness, human compassion or personal remorse; exhibits a coarse uncivility, as well as an offensive, if not ruthless, indifference to the welfare of others.

TABLE 11 *(cont.)*
Mood/Temperament Domain

Personality *(cont.)*	
Sadistic	Hostile: has an excitable and pugnacious temper which flares readily into contentious argument and phsyical belligerance; is mean-spirited and fractious, willing to do harm, even persecute others, to get one's way.
Compulsive	Solemn: is unrelaxed, tense, joyless and grim; restrains warm feelings and keeps most emotions under tight control.
Passive-Aggressive	Irritable: frequently touchy, obstinate, and resentful, followed in turn by sulky and moody withdrawal; is often fretful and impatient, reporting being easily annoyed or frustrated by others.
Self-Defeating	Doleful: is frequently forlorn and mournful; will intentionally display a plaintive and gloomy appearance, occasionally to induce guilt and discomfort in others.
Schizotypal	Distraught or Insentient: reports being apprehensive and ill-at-ease, particularly in social encounters; is agitated and axiously watchful, distrustful of others and wary of their motives; *or* manifests drab, apathetic, sluggish, joyless, and spiritless appearance; reveals marked deficiencies in face-to-face rapport and emotional expression.
Borderline	Labile: fails to accord unstable mood level with external reality; has either marked shifts from normality to depression to excitement, or has extended periods of dejection and apathy, interspersed with brief spells of anger, anxiety, or euphoria.
Paranoid	Irascible: displays a cold, sullen, churlish, and humorless demeanor; attempts to appear unemotional and objective, but is edgy, envious, jealous, quick to react angrily, or take personal offense.

expressive acts, interpersonal conduct, cognitive style, self-image, and mood/temperament, a narrower scope of attributes than desirable, but one sufficient to provide a reasonably comprehensive picture of a patient's major characteristics.

The MPTQ self-report not only introduces a means by which the bipolar components of the evolutionary model can be quantified, but also supplies a tool for determining individual personality style profiles among nonclinical populations. Together with the MPDC and the MCMI-II, these new instruments equip both clinicians and researchers with a set of implements to evaluate the theory they share in common.

CHAPTER SIX

INTERVENTION

Integrative Therapy for Personality Disorders

*T*he Spanish scholar Ortega y Gasset puts it that the
man of antiquity, before he did anything, took a step
backwards, like the bullfighter who leaps back to deliver a
mortal thrust. He searched the past for a pattern into
which he might slip as into a diving-bell, and being thus
at once disguised and protected might rush upon his
present problem (Mann, 1937).

A major treatment implication recorded in prior chapters noted that the polarity schema and clinical domains can serve as useful points of focus for corresponding modalities of therapy. It would be ideal, of course, if patients were "pure" prototypes, and all polarities prototypal and invariably present. Were this so, each diagnosis would automatically match with its polarity configuration and corresponding therapeutic mode. Unfortunately, "real" patients rarely are pure textbook prototypes; most, by far, are complex mixtures, exhibiting, for example, the deficient pain and pleasure polarities that typify the schizoid prototype, the interpersonal conduct and cognitive style features of the avoidant prototype, the self-image qualities that characterize the schizotypal, and so on. Further, the polarity configurations and their expressive domains are not likely to be of equal clinical relevance or prominence in a particular case; thus, the interpersonal characteristics may be especially troublesome, whereas cognitive processes, though problematic, may be of lesser significance. Which domains and which polarities should be selected for therapeutic intervention is not, therefore, merely a matter of making "a diagnosis," but requires a comprehensive assessment, one that appraises not only the overall configuration of polarities and domains, but differentiates their balance and degrees of salience.

Before turning to substantive therapeutic matters, a brief comment on a few philosophical issues is necessary. These issues bear on a rationale for developing theory-based treatment techniques and methods, that is, methods that transcend the merely empirical (e.g., electroconvulsive therapy for depressives). Also noted, somewhat briefly is an epistemologically spurious issue found in its most obtuse form in debates concerning which treatment orientation (cognitive, behavioral, biologic, intrapsychic) is "closer to the truth," or which therapeutic method is intrinsically the more efficacious.

What differentiates these treatment orientations has little to do with either their theoretical underpinnings or their empirical support, but to the fact that they limit their attention to different clinical domains. Their differences are akin to physicists, chemists, and biologists arguing over which field was a truer representation of nature. It is to the credit of those of an eclectic persuasion that they have recognized the arbitrary if not illogical character of such contentions, as well as the need to bridge schisms that have been constructed less by philosophical considerations, theoretic logic, or pragmatic goals than by the accidents of history and professional rivalries.

Although integrative therapy approaches can be applied to a variety of diverse clinical conditions, it would be wise to outline some reasons why personality disorders are that segment of psychopathology for which integrative psychotherapy is ideally and distinctively suited—in the same sense as behavioral techniques appear most efficacious in the modification of problematic actions, cognitive methods optimal for reframing phenomenological distortions, and intrapsychic techniques especially apt in resolving unconscious processes.

The cohesion (or lack thereof) of complexly interwoven psychic structures and functions is what distinguishes the disorders of personality from other clinical syndromes; likewise, the orchestration of diverse, yet synthesized techniques of intervention is what differentiates integrative from other variants of psychotherapy. These two, parallel constructs, emerging from different traditions and conceived in different venues, reflect shared philosophical perspectives, one oriented toward the understanding of psychopathology, the other toward effecting its remediation.

It is not that integrative therapies are inapplicable to more focal pathologies but rather that these therapies are *required* for the personality disorders (whereas depression may successfully be treated either cognitively or pharmacologically); it is the very interwoven nature of the components that comprise personality disorders that make a multifaceted approach a necessity.

It should be noted, however, that much of what travels under the "eclectic" or "integrative" banner sounds like the talk of a "goody two shoes"—a desire to be nice to all sides, and to say that everybody is right. These labels have become platitudinous buzzwords, philosophies with which open-minded people certainly would wish to ally themselves. But "integrative psychotherapy," at least as it should be applied to the personality disorders, must signify more than that.

First, it is more than eclecticism; perhaps it should be termed posteclecticism, if we may borrow a characterization of modern art a century ago. Eclecticism should not be a matter of choice. We all must be eclectics, engaging in differential (Frances et al., 1984) and multimodal (Lazarus, 1981) therapeutics, selecting the techniques that are empirically the most efficacious for the problems at hand. Second, integration is more than the coexistence of two or three previously discordant orientations or techniques. We cannot piece together the odds and ends of several theoretical schemas, each internally consistent and oriented to different data domains and expect them to cohere. Such a hodgepodge will lead only to illusory syntheses that cannot long hold together. Efforts such as these, meritorious as they may be in some regards, represent the work of peacemakers, not innovators and not therapeutic integrationists.

The integration labeled "personologic psychotherapy" (Millon, 1988) insists on the primacy of an overarching gestalt that gives coherence, provides an interactive framework, and creates an organic order among otherwise discrete polarities and attributes. It is eclectic, of course, but more. It is synthesized from a substantive theory whose overall utility and orientation derives from that old chestnut: The whole is greater than the sum of its parts. As we know well, the personality problems our patients bring to us are an inextricably linked nexus of interpersonal behaviors, cognitive styles, regulatory processes, and so on. They flow through a tangle of feedback loops and serially unfolding concatenations that emerge at different times in dynamic and changing configurations. Each component of these configurations has its role and significance altered by virtue of its place in these continually evolving constellations. In parallel form, so should personologic psychotherapy be conceived as an integrated configuration of strategies and tactics in which each intervention technique is selected *not only* for its efficacy in resolving particular pathological attributes but also for its contribution to the overall constellation of treatment procedures of which it is but one.

Besides the author's obvious bias, why should personality factors be emphasized in psychotherapy? One view is that at the center of all therapies, whether we work with "part functions" that focus on behaviors, or cognitions, or unconscious processes, defects, and the like, *or* whether we address contextual systems which focus on the psychosocial environment, the family, the group, or the socioeconomic conditions of life, the crossover point, the place that links parts to contexts is the person, the individual, the intersecting medium that brings them together.

But persons are more than just crossover mediums. As we stated earlier, persons are the only organically integrated system in the psychological domain, inherently created from birth as natural entities, rather than experience-derived gestalts constructed via cognitive attribution. Moreover, persons lie at the heart of the psychotherapeutic experience, the substantive beings that give meaning and coherence to symptoms and traits—be they behaviors, affects, or mechanisms—as well as those beings that experience and express what transpires in family interactions and social processes.

The new breed of integrative and eclectic therapists should take cognizance of the person from the start, for the parts and the contexts take on different meanings, and call for different interventions in terms of the person to whom they are anchored. To focus on one social structure or one psychic form of expression, without understanding its undergirding or reference base is to engage in potentially misguided, if not random, therapeutic techniques.

Although the admonition that we should not employ the same therapeutic approach with all patients is self-evident, it appears that therapeutic approaches accord more with where training occurred than with the nature of the patients' pathologies. To paraphrase (Millon, 1969), there continues to be a disinclination among clinical practitioners to submit their cherished techniques to detailed study or to revise them in line with critical empirical findings. Despite the fact that most of our therapeutic research leaves much to be desired in the way of proper controls, sampling, and evaluative criteria, one overriding fact comes through repeatedly: Therapeutic techniques must be suited to the patient's problem. Simple and obvious though this statement is, it is repeatedly neglected by therapists who persist in utilizing and argue heatedly in favor of *a* particular approach to *all* variants of psychopathology. No "school" of therapy is exempt from this notorious attitude.

Why should we formulate an integrated therapeutic strategy with the personality disorders? The answer may perhaps be best grasped if we think of the polarities of personality as analogous to the sections of an orchestra, and the clinical attributes of a patient as a clustering of discordant instruments that exhibit imbalances, deficiencies, or conflicts within these sections. To extend this analogy, therapists may be seen as conductors whose task is to bring forth a harmonious balance among all the sections, as well as their specifically discordant instruments, muting some here, accentuating others there, all to the end of fulfilling the conductor's knowledge of how "the composition" can best be made consonant. The task is not that of altering one instrument, but of all, *in concert*. What is sought in music, then, is a balanced score, one composed of harmonic counterpoints, rhythmic patterns, and melodic combinations. What is needed in therapy is a likewise balanced program, a coordinated strategy of counterpoised techniques designed to optimize sequential and combinatorial treatment effects.

To be more concrete, consider, for example, what makes personologic therapy integrated, rather than eclectic?

In the latter, there is a separateness among techniques, just a wise selectivity of what works best. In personologic therapy there are psychologically designed composites and progressions among diverse techniques. In an attempt to formulate them in current writings (Millon, 1988), terms such as "catalytic sequences" and "potentiating pairings" are employed to represent the nature and intent of these polarity-oriented and attribute-focused treatment plans. In essence, they comprise therapeutic arrangements and timing series which promote polarity balances and effect attribute changes that would otherwise not occur by the use of only one technique.

In a "catalytic sequence," for example, one might seek first to alter a patient's humiliating and *pain*ful stuttering by direct modification procedures which, if achieved, may facilitate the use of cognitive methods in producing *self*-image changes in confidence which may, in its turn, foster the utility of interpersonal techniques in effecting improvements in relationships with *others*. In "potentiated pairing" one may simultaneously combine, as is commonly done these days, both behavioral and cognitive methods so as to overcome problematic interactions with *others* and conceptions of *self* that might be refractory to either technique alone.

A defining feature of personality disorders is that they are themselves pathogenic; Millon described this process as "self-perpetuation" (1969); Horney (1937) characterized it earlier in her use of the concept of "vicious circles"; Wachtel (1977) has suggested the term "cyclical psychodynamics." It is these ceaseless and entangled sequences of repetitive cognitions, interpersonal behaviors, and unconscious mechanisms that call for the use of simultaneous or alternately focused methods. The synergism and enhancement produced by such catalytic and potentiating processes is what comprise genuine personologic strategies.

As a general philosophy then, it seems that we should select our specific treatment techniques only as tactics to achieve polarity-oriented goals. Depending on the pathological polarity and domains to be modified, and the overall treatment sequence one has in mind, the goals of therapy should be oriented toward the improvement of imbalanced or deficient polarities by the use of techniques that are optimally suited to modify their expression in those clinical domains that are problematic.

Table 12 provides a synopsis of what may be considered the primary goals of personologic therapy according to the polarity model. Therapeutic efforts responsive to problems in the *pain-pleasure* polarity would, for example, have as their essential aim the enhancement of pleasure among schizoid and avoidant personalities (+ pleasure). Given the probability of intrinsic deficits in this area, schizoids might require the use of pharmacologic agents designed to activate their "flat" mood/temperament. Increments in pleasure for avoidants, however,

TABLE 12
Polarity-Oriented Personologic Therapy

Modifying the Pain-Pleasure Polarity
+ Pleasure (Schizoid/Avoidant)   − Pain (Avoidant)   Pain↔Pleasure (Self-Defeating/Sadistic)
Balancing the Passive-Active Polarity
+ Passive − Active (Avoidant/Histrionic/Antisocial/Sadistic/Passive-Aggressive)   − Passive + Active (Schizoid/Dependent/Narcissistic/Self-Defeating/Compulsive)
Altering the Other-Self Polarity
− Other + Self (Dependent/Histrionic)   + Other − Self (Narcissistic/Antisocial)   Other ↔ Self (Compulsive/Passive-Aggressive)
Rebuilding the Personality Structure
+ Cognitive/Interpersonal Cohesion (Schizotypal)   + Affective/Self Cohesion (Borderline)   − Cognitive/Affective Cohesion (Paranoid)

are likely to depend more on cognitive techniques designed to alter their "alienated" self-image, and behavioral methods oriented to counter their "aversive" interpersonal inclinations. Equally important for avoidants is reducing their hypersensitivities especially to social rejection (− pain); this may be achieved by coordinating the use of medications for their characteristic "anguished" mood/temperament with cognitive methods geared to desensitization. In the *passive-active* polarity, increments in the capacity and skills to take a less reactive and more proactive role in dealing with the affairs of their lives (− passive; + active) would be a major goal of treatment for schizoids, dependents, narcissists, self-defeatists, and compulsives. Turning to the *other-self* polarity, imbalances found among narcissists and antisocials, for example, suggest that a major aim of their treatment would be a reduction in their predominant self-focus, and a corresponding augmentation of their sensitivity to the needs of others (+ other; − self).

To make unbalanced or deficient polarities the primary aim of therapy is a new focus and a goal as yet untested. In contrast, the clinical domains in which problems are expressed lend themselves to a wide variety of therapeutic techniques, the efficacy of which must, of course, continue to be gauged by ongoing experience and future systematic research. Nevertheless, our repertoire here is a rich one. For example, there are numerous behavior modification techniques (Bandura, 1969; Goldfried & Davison, 1976), such as assertiveness training, that may fruitfully be employed to establish a greater sense of *self* autonomy or an *active* rather than a *passive* stance with regard to life. Similarly, pharmaceuticals are notably efficacious in reducing the intensity of *pain* (anxiety, depression) when the pleasure-pain polarity is in marked imbalance.

Turning to the specific domains in which clinical problems exhibit themselves, we can address dysfunctions in the realm of "interpersonal conduct" by employing any number of family (Gurman and Kniskern, 1981) or group (Yalom, 1986) therapeutic methods, as well as a series of recently evolved and explicitly formulated interpersonal techniques (Anchin & Kiesler, 1982). Methods of classical analysis or its more contemporary schools may be especially suited to the realm of "object representations," as would the methods of Beck (1976), Ellis (1970), and Meichenbaum (1977) be well chosen to modify difficulties of "cognitive style" and "self image."

The goals, as well as the strategies and modes of action, for when and how one might practice personologic therapy have only begun to be specified.

EPILOGUE

Closing Reflections

*T*he dramatic quality of insight, born in an ecstasy or in
an agony of creative intensity, often leads the artist to
forget that the baby must still be brought up. The toil may
be arduous, for a great deal has to be changed completely;
indeed, the painting or drama may take a constantly
changing form, and there may be many further insights
along the way. The quality of mind is shown nearly as
much in the capacity for masterful polishing as in the gift
of sudden illumination. Literary and artistic history, and
the history of science and invention, are strewn with the
wreckage of . . . ideas not carried through (Murphy, 1947).

Has this book succeeded in honoring the creative spirit that characterized the life and work of Gardner Murphy and Henry Murray? Has it contributed to breaking what may be the insecure empiricism that has narrowed the vision and led to the patchwork quilt of unrelated domains that characterize our field today?

As is evident, this work tries to emulate not only Murphy and Murray's personologic themes and ambitions, but also their steadfast view that we must press beyond proximate boundaries and explore hypotheses that derive their principles and substance from adjacent and more established sciences. I believe both Murphy and Murray would have found it congenial to conceive the matrix of personality traits and disorders to be susceptible to explanation within an evolutionary framework. Both shared the mindset of those who opted for cohesion rather than discontinuity, for unification rather than discreteness, for cohering schemas and integrating constructs that link the several domains of nature's expression.

If my own effort to keep pace with Murphy's scope and Murray's fertility has fallen short, it is that this brief work has omitted much, and that the synthesis sought has excluded too many spheres of nature's phenomena. Fortunately, history tells us that the wisdom of exclusion is not determined by a priori decisions but rather results from unsuccessful attempts to make all matters of nature's puzzle fit well together. Short as this book has been, it would have been more presumptuous to have pushed it beyond its already speculative reach. Nonetheless, it is but a brief and perhaps less than optimal sketch of what I believe will continue to be a fruitful synthesis of evolutionary biology and personology. As an introduction, perhaps it will serve to whet the appetite of the serious and open-minded reader.

Before closing my argument favoring the congruence of personologic and evolutionary theory, let me state that I agree with those who distinguish two major trends in personology—those who believe that advances in the science will occur by the accumulation of empirical data and those who see growth occurring through the use of illuminating explanatory schemas. The former derive data from palpable clinical and research observations, stating their findings and hypotheses in the language of behavioral observables; the latter employ theoretical constructs to describe and articulate underlying principles that give meaning to personologic structures and functions. This broad epistemological dichotomy was first drawn by Aristotle when he sought to contrast the understanding of diseases with reference to knowledge of principles—which ostensibly deal with all instances of a disease, however diverse—versus direct empirical knowledge—which deals presumably only with specific and tangible instances. To Aristotle, knowledge based on direct, empirical experience alone represented a more primitive type of knowledge than that informed by a conceptual theory which could, through the application of principles, explain not only why a particular disease occurs, but illuminate commonalities among seemingly diverse ailments. This same theme was raised in the writings of the distinguished nineteenth century neurologist, Hughlings Jackson. For example, Jackson drew a distinction between two kinds of disease classifications, one "scientific," which he termed theoretical, designed to advance the state of knowledge, the other "empirical," which he termed clinical, and was organized for routine or daily practice. Both were seen as necessary, but Jackson asserted that with each elucidation of a contemporary disease there would be an accretion of theory, resulting in the ultimate supplanting of "mere" clinical knowledge.

A more recent and parallel distinction has been drawn between "manifest" and "scientific" images in diagnostic practice (Sellars, 1963). For example, direct encounters between a diagnostician and a patient initially evoke a manifest image;

that is, a subjective and sensory impression of their shared experiences in that particular context. Events of this nature are immediate and phenomenological. By contrast, scientific images are a product of a screening process in which events are modified by filters and mental constructs that transform the immediacy of "natural" experience in terms of theory-derived concepts and preestablished objective evidence. Differing from the experiential quality of the manifest world, scientific images may seem remote in that they reflect implicit theoretical formulations, gaining their evidential support from esoteric and arcane sources.

The contrast between manifest and scientific images reflects in part one of philosophy's more perennial problems; namely, the rivalry between opposing views regarding the primary source of knowledge (e. g., the empiricist versus rationalist epistemologies). Rationalism argues not only that knowledge consists of principles and universals, but that knowledge is what distinguishes the mind from the senses, the latter being capable of apprehending only experiential particulars. In rebuttal, empiricists contend that knowledge must be derived from direct sensory experience first, and only then generalized to broader principles. Rationalists assert in response that it is the logic of reasoning that distinguishes the human from lower species.

Medicine has been rent throughout its history by this empiricist-rationalist dichotomy. Debates between Aristotelian and Galenic rationalist exponents, on the one hand, and Hippocratic and Paracelsian empiricists, on the other, led to repeated, if not consistent, disagreement as how diseases should be characterized and understood. This very issue continues as we seek to conceptualize and organize personology today. Shall we follow the policy guiding the construction of the *DSM*, an empiricist-clinical approach, or should we assume an orientation more consonant with a rationalist-theoretical formulation?

A few more words should be said about the role of theoretical constructs in generating nosologies. As noted earlier, distinguished philosophers such as Hempel (1965) and Quine (1977) consider that mature sciences progress from an observationally based stage to one that is characterized by abstract concepts and theoretical systemizations. It is their judgment that classification alone does not make a scientific taxonomy, and that similarity among attributes does not necessarily comprise a scientific category. The card catalog of the library or an accountant's ledger sheet, for example, are well-organized classifications, but hardly to be viewed as a system of science. The characteristic which distinguishes a scientific classification, or what we term a latent as contrasted to a manifest taxonomy, is its success in grouping its elements according to theoretically consonant explanatory propositions. The propositions are formed when certain attributes which have been isolated and categorized have been shown or have been hypothesized to be logically or causally related to other attributes or categories. The latent diagnostic classes comprising a nosology are not, therefore, mere collections of overtly similar attributes or categories, but a linked or unified pattern of known or presumed relationships among them. This theoretically grounded pattern of relationships is the foundation of a scientific taxonomy.

One more comment: Theories need be neither fully comprehensive nor extensively supported to inspire and guide the early phases of nosologic development. Addressing these points in discussing his concept of the schizoid category, Meehl wrote (1972):

> I would not require that a genuinely integrated theory explain *everything* about schizophrenia, a preposterous demand, which we do not customarily make of any theory in the biological or social sciences. At this stage of our knowledge, it is probably bad strategy to spend time theorizing about small effects, low correlations, minor discrepancies between studies and the like.
>
> Being a neo-Popperian in the philosophy of science, I am myself quite comfortable engaging in speculative

formulations completely unsubstantiated by data. To "justify" concocting a theory, all one needs is a problem, plus a notion (I use a weak word advisedly) of how one might test one's theory (subject it to the danger of refutation) (p. 11).

The reader may be taken aback by Meehl's seemingly tolerant views, and be disposed to assert that theory leads to scientific irresponsibility, justifying thereby the taking of a rigorous atheoretical stance. As we have stated previously, however, the belief that one can take positions that are free of theoretical bias is naive, if not nonsensical. Those who claim to have eschewed theory have (unknowingly) subscribed to a position that gives primacy to experience-near data, such as overt behaviors and biological signs, as opposed to experience-distant data that require a greater measure of inference. The positivist (empiricist) position once held sway in philosophy, as it still does in some psychiatric and psychological quarters, but it would be difficult, as Meehl (1978) has noted, "to name a single logician or a philosopher (or historian) of science who today defends strict operationism in the sense that some psychologists claim to believe in it" (p. 815).

Personology employed biological and social learning principles in my early writings (Millon, 1969). These biosocial foundations have not been dispensed with nor denied significance as explanatory constructs. An exploration of the topic from the perspective of evolutionary principles revealed, however, that certain opacities narrowed my biosocial analyses. No less important, evolutionary conceptualizations anchored the field of personology to a firmly grounded body of scientific knowledge, rather than left to drift on its own, an isolated discipline and level of inquiry.

Theorists, of course, are skilled at a priori reasoning; for the most part their formulations are rarely tarnished by the realities of everyday clinical practice. The "real job" that faces most theorists is that of keeping their conceptions simple and generalizable enough to provide useful insights to the practicing clinician. No less important, they must maintain sufficient distance not to "fall in love" with their own formulations, as if they embodied some ultimate "truth." I trust in this regard that I have not misled the reader by virtue of authorial vanity or theoretical obsession. Likewise, it is hoped the reader who has progressed to this final segment of the book has not developed a hardening of the spirit of inquiry, a loss of those imaginative outreachings that open one to fresh, albeit conjectural theses.

Some may very well argue they just struggled through an author's need not only to impose an unnecessary order but to frame its elements in an overly formalistic sequence, that I, the author, have forced the subject of personology into the procrustean bed of theoretical predilections, drawing on tangential topics of little or no relevance. If such a case be valid, I regret that my habit of seeking bridges between scientific domains has led me to cohere subjects best left disparate. It is hoped that this philosophic prejudice, obviously inspired by a personally driven world view, will yet prove to have a modicum of empirical merit and theoretical value.

To be at all successful, this brief volume should furnish an "image," if you will, one analogous to the clockwork portrayal fashioned in Newton's synthesis of nature's forces, an image whose appeal derives from its reflection of the deepest antitheses of physical and biologic evolution, and the recognition that these very same antitheses are to be found, as well, in the quandaries and agonies of human nature.

References

Abelson, R., and Sermat V. (1962). Multidimensional scaling of facial expressions. *Journal of Experimental Psychology, 63*, 546–554.

American Psychiatric Association (1980). *Diagnostic and statistical manual of mental disorders.* 3rd ed. *DSM-III.* Washington, DC: Author.

American Psychiatric Association (1987). *Diagnostic and statistical manual of mental disorders.* 3rd ed. revised *(DSM-III-R).* Washington, DC: Author.

Anchin, J. C., and Kiesler, D. J., eds. (1982). *Handbook of interpersonal psychotherapy.* New York: Pergamon.

Angyal, A. (1941). *Foundations for a science of personality.* New York: Commonwealth Fund.

Bandura, A. (1969). *Principles of behavior modification.* New York: Holt, Rinehart & Winston.

Bandura, A. (1977). *Social learning theory.* Englewood Cliffs, NJ: Prentice-Hall.

Barash, D. P. (1977). *Sociobiology and behavior.* New York: Elsevier.

Barash, D. P. (1982). *Sociobiology and behavior.* 2nd ed. New York: Elsevier.

Barash, D. P. (1986). *The hare and the tortoise.* New York: Viking.

Beck, A. T. (1976). *Cognitive therapy and the emotional disorders.* New York: International Universities Press.

Beck, A. T.; Epstein, N.: and Harrison, R. P. (1988). Development of the sociotropy-autonomy scale: A measure of personality factors in psychopathology. Unpublished manuscript. Philadelphia: University of Pennsylvania.

Benjamin, L. S. (1974). Structural analysis of social behavior. *Psychological Review, 81*, 392–425.

Benjamin, L. S. (1984). Principles of prediction using structural analysis of social behavior. In. R. A. Zucker, J. Aronoff, and A. I.

Rabin, eds. *Personality and the Prediction of Behavior*. New York: Academic Press.

Benjamin, L. S. (1986). Adding social and intrapsychic descriptors to Axis I of DSM-III. In T. Millon and G. L. Klerman eds., *Contemporary Directions in Psychopathology*. New York: Guilford.

Bertalanffy, L. von (1945). *Problems of life*. New York: Wiley.

Blatt, S. J., and Shichman, S. (1983). Two primary configurations of psychopathology. *Psychoanalysis and Contemporary Thought, 6,* 187–254.

Bowers, K. S. (1977). There's more to Iago than meets the eye: A clinical account of personal consistency. In D. Magnusson and N. S. Endler, eds., *Personality at the Crossroads*. Hillsdale, NJ: Erlbaum.

Buss, A. H. (1987). Personality: Primitive heritage and human distinctiveness. In J. Aronoff, A. I. Rabin, and R. A. Zucker, eds., *The Emergence of Personality*. New York: Springer.

Buss, A. H., and Plomin, R. (1975). *A Temperament theory of personality development*. New York: Wiley.

Buss, A. J., and Plomin R. (1984). *Temperament: early developing personality traits*. Hillsdale, NJ: Erlbaum.

Buss, D. M. (1984). Evolutionary biology and personality psychology. *American Psychologist, 39,* 1135–1147.

Cannon, W. (1927). *Bodily changes in pain, hunger, fear and rage*. New York: Appleton-Century-Crofts.

Cannon, W. (1939). *The wisdom of the body*. New York: Norton.

Chodorow, N. (1974). Family structure and feminine personality. In M. Rosaldo and L. Lamphere, eds., *Women, Culture, and Society*. Stanford: Stanford University Press.

Chodorow, N. (1978). *The reproduction of mothering*. Berkeley: University of California Press.

Cloninger, C. R. (1986). A unified biosocial theory of personality and its role in the development of anxiety states. *Psychiatric Developments, 3,* 167–226.

Cloninger, C. R. (1987). A systematic method for clinical description and classification of personality variants. *Archives of General Psychiatry, 44,* 573–588.

Cole, L. C. (1954). The population consequences of life history phenomena. *Quarterly Review of Biology, 29,* 103–137.

Daly, M., and Wilson, M. (1978). *Sex, evolution and behavior*. Boston: Grant Press.

Darwin, C. R. (1859). *On the origin of species by means of natural selection.* London: Murray.

Darwin, C. R. (1871). *The descent of man and selection in relation to sex.* London: Murray.

Duffy, E. (1957). The psychological significance of the concept of "arousal" or "activation." *Psychological Review, 64,* 265–275.

Eldredge, N., and Gould, S. (1972). Punctuated equilibria: An alternative to phyletic gradualism. In T. Schopf, ed., *Models in Paleobiology.* San Francisco: Freeman.

Ellis, A. (1970). *The essence of rational psychotherapy: A comprehensive approach to treatment.* New York: Institute for Rational Living.

Everly, G. (1988). The biological basis of personality: The contribution of paleocortical anatomy and physiology. Paper presented at the First International Congress on Disorders of Personality, Copenhagen, Denmark, August 1988.

Eysenck, H. J. (1957). *The dynamics of anxiety and hysteria.* London: Routledge & Paul.

Eysenck, H. J. (1967). *The biological basis of personality.* Springfield, IL: Thomas.

Eysenck, H. J., ed. (1981). *A model for personality.* New York: Springer-Verlag.

Fairbairn, W. R. D. (1954). *An object relations theory of personality.* New York: Basic Books.

Feldman, R., and Quenzar, L. (1984). *Fundamentals of neuropharmacology.* Sunderland, MA: Sinauer.

Fenichel, O. (1945). *The psychoanalytic theory of neurosis.* New York: Norton.

Foa, U. G., and Foa, E. B. (1974). *Social structures of the mind.* Springfield, IL: Thomas.

Frances, A.; Clarkin, J.; and Perry, S. (1984). *Differential therapeutics in psychiatry.* New York: Brunner/Mazel.

Freud, A. (1965). *Normality and pathology of childhood: Assessments of development.* New York: International Universities Press.

Freud, S. (1895). *Project for a scientific psychology.* In *Standard Edition* (English translation, vol. 1). London: Hogarth.

Freud, S. (1905). Three essays on the theory of sexuality. In *Standard Edition* (English translation, vol. 7). London: Hogarth.

Freud, S. (1914/1925). On narcissism: An introduction. In *Collected Papers* (vol. 4). London: Hogarth.

Freud, S. (1915/1925). The instincts and their vicissitudes. In *Collected Papers* (vol. 4). London: Hogarth.

Freud, S. (1940). *An outline of psychoanalysis.* New York: Liveright.

Garai, J., and Scheinfeld, A. (1968). Sex differences in mental traits. *Genetic Psychology Monographs, 77,* 169–299.

Gill, M. M. (1963). *Topography and systems in psychoanalytic theory.* New York: International Universities Press.

Gilligan, C. (1981). *In a different voice.* Cambridge, MA: Harvard University Press.

Gleick, J. (1987). *Chaos: Making a new science.* New York: Viking.

Goldberg, A., ed. (1978). *The psychology of self: A casebook.* New York: International Universities Press.

Goldberg, A., ed. (1985). *Progress in self psychology* (vol. 1). New York: Guilford.

Goldfried, M., and Davison, G. (1976). *Clinical behavior therapy.* New York: Holt, Rinehart & Winston.

Gray, J. (1982). *The neuropsychology of anxiety.* Oxford: Oxford Universities Press.

Gray, J. A., ed. (1964). *Pavlov's typology.* New York: Pergamon.

Gray, J. A. (1973). Causal theories of personality and how to test them. In J. R. Royce, Ed., *Multivariate Analysis and Psychological Theory.* New York: Academic Press.

Gray, J. A. (1975). *Elements of a two-process theory of learning.* New York: Academic Press.

Gray, J. A. (1981). A critique of Eysenck's theory of personality. In H. J. Eysenck, Ed., *A Model for Personality.* New York: Springer-Verlag.

Green, R., and Cliff, N. (1975). Multidimensional comparisons of structures of vocally and facially expressed emotions. *Perceptions and Psychophysics, 17,* 429–438.

Gribbin, J. (1986). *In search of the big bang.* Toronto: Bantam.

Gurman, A. S., and Kniskern, D., eds. (1981). *The handbook of family therapy.* New York: Brunner/Mazel.

Hall, J. (1978). Gender effects in decoding nonverbal cues. *Psychological Bulletin, 85,* 845–857.

Hamilton, W. D. (1964). The genetical evolution of social behavior: I and II. *Journal of Theoretical Biology, 7,* 1–52.

Hartmann, H. (1939). *Ego psychology and the problem of adaption.* New York: International Universities Press.

Haviland, J., and Malatesta, C. (1981). The development of sex differences in nonverbal signals. In C. Mayo and N. Henley, eds., *Gender and Nonverbal Behavior.* New York: Springer.

Hebb, D. O. (1949). *The organization of behavior.* New York: Wiley.

Hebb, D. O. (1955). Drives and the C. N. S. (Conceptual Nervous System). *Psychological Review, 62,* 243–254.

Hempel, C. G. (1961). Introduction to problems of taxonomy. In J. Zubin, ed., *Field Studies in the Mental Disorders.* New York: Grune & Stratton.

Hempel, C. G. (1965). *Aspects of scientific explanation.* New York: Free Press.

Henry, J. P., and Stephens, P. (1977). *Stress, health, and the social environment.* New York: Springer-Verlag.

Horney, K. (1926/1967). The flight from womanhood. In H. Kelman, ed., *Feminine Psychology.* New York: Norton.

Horney, K. (1937). *The neurotic personality of our time.* New York: Norton.

Huxley, T. H. (1870). Mr. Darwin's critics. *Contemporary Review, 18,* 443–476.

Ivanov-Smolensky, A. G. (1953). The study of types of higher nervous system activity in animals and man. *Zhurnal Vysshei Nervnoi Deyatelnosti, 3,* 36–54.

Jacobson, E. (1964). *The self and the object world.* New York: International Universities Press.

Kendall, R. E. (1975). *The role of diagnosis in psychiatry.* Oxford: Blackwell.

Kernberg, O. (1975). *Borderline conditions and pathological narcissism.* New York: Jason Aronson.

Kernberg, O. (1976). *Object relations theory and clinical psychoanalysis.* New York: Jason Aronson.

Kernberg, O. (1980). *Internal world and external reality.* New York: Jason Aronson.

Kernberg, O. (1984). *Severe personality disorders.* New Haven: Yale University Press.

Kiesler, D. J. (1986). The 1982 interpersonal circle: An analysis of DSM-III personality disorders. In T. Millon and G. L. Klerman, eds., *Contemporary Directions in Psychopathology.* New York: Guilford.

Klein, M. (1952). *Developments in psychoanalysis.* London: Hogarth Press.

Kluver, H., and Bucy, P. (1939). Preliminary analysis of functions of the temporal lobes in monkeys. *Archives of Neurology and Psychiatry, 42,* 979–1000.

Kohut, H. (1971). *The analysis of self.* New York: International Universities Press.

Kohut, H. (1977). *The restoration of the self.* New York: International Universities Press.

Korner, A. (1969). Neonatal startles, smiles, erections, and reflex sucks as related to state, age, and individuality. *Child Development, 40,* 1039–1053.

Korner, A. (1973). Sex differences in newborns with special reference to differences in the organization of oral behavior. *Journal of Child Psychology and Psychiatry, 14,* 19–29.

Kraepelin, E. (1899). *Psychiatrie: Ein lehrbuch,* 6th ed. Leipzig: Barth.

Krasnogorsky, N. I. (1958). *Studies in higher nervous activity of Man and Animals.* (vol. 1). Moscow: Medgiz.

Lawrence, D. H. (1921). *Psychoanalysis and the unconscious.* London: Routledge & Paul.

Lazarus, A. A. (1981). *The practice of multimodal therapy.* New York: McGraw-Hill.

Leary, T. (1957). *Interpersonal diagnosis of personality.* New York: Ronald Press.

Lewis, M. (1969). Infant's responses to facial stimuli during the first year of life. *Developmental Psychology, 1,* 75–86.

Lewontin, R. C. (1979). Sociobiology as an adaptationist program. *Behavioral Science, 24,* 5–14.

Lindsley, D. B. (1951). Emotion. In S. S. Stevens, ed., *Handbook of Experimental Psychology.* New York: Wiley.

Lotka, A. J. (1924). *Elements of mathematical biology.* New York: Dover.

Lynn, D. (1961). Sex role and parental identification. *Child Development, 33,* 555–564.

Maccoby, E., and Jacklin, C. (1974). *The psychology of sex differences.* Stanford: Stanford University Press.

MacLean, P. (1949). Psychosomatic disease and the "visceral brain." *Psychosomatic Medicine. 11,* 338–353.

MacLean, P. (1952). Some psychiatric implications of physiologic studies on frontotemporal portions of the limbic system. *Electro-encephalography and Clinical Neuropysiology, 4,* 407–418.

MacLean, P. (1985). Brain evolution relating to family, play, and the separation call. *Archives of General Psychiatry, 42,* 405–417.

MacLean, P. (1986). Culminating developments in the evolution of the limbic system. In B. Doane and K. Livingston, eds., *The Limbic System.* New York: Raven Press.

Mandelbrot, B. (1977). *The fractal geometry of nature.* New York: Freeman.

Mann, T. (1937). *Freud, Goethe and Wagner.* New York: Norton.

Mayr, E. (1964). The evolution of living systems. *Proceedings of the National Academy of Science, 51,* 934–941.

McAdams, D. P. (1985). A life-story model of identity. In R. Hogan and W. Jones, eds., *Perspectives in Personality.* New York: Plenum.

McDougall, W. (1908). *Introduction to social psychology.* New York: Scribners.

McNair, D. M., and Lorr, M. (1964). An analysis of mood in neurotics. *Journal of Abnormal and Social Psychology, 69,* 620–627.

Mead, M. (1949). *Male and female.* New York: Norton.

Meehl, P. (1972). Specific genetic etiology, psychodynamics, and therapeutic nihilism. *International Journal of Mental Health, 1,* 10–27.

Meehl, P. (1978). Theoretical risks and tabular asterisks: Sir Karl, Sir Ronald, and the slow progress of soft psychology. *Journal of Consulting and Clinical Psychology, 46,* 806–834.

Meichenbaum, D. (1977). *Cognitive-behavioral modification.* New York: Plenum.

Millon, T., ed. (1967). *Theories of psychopathology.* Philadelphia: Saunders.

Millon, T. (1969). *Modern psychopathology.* Philadelphia: Saunders (reprinted, 1985. Prospect Heights, IL: Waveland Press).

Millon, T. (1981). *Disorders of personality: DSM-III, Axis II.* New York: Wiley-Interscience.

Millon, T. (1983). The DSM-III: An insider's perspective. *American Psychologist, 38,* 804–814.

Millon, T. (1984). On the renaissance of personality assessment and personality theory. *Journal of Personality Assessment, 48,* 450–466.

Millon, T. (1986a). A theoretical derivation of pathological personalities. In T. Millon and G. Klerman, eds., *Contemporary Directions in Psychopathology*. New York: Guilford.

Millon, T. (1986b). Personality prototypes and their diagnostic criteria. In T. Millon and G. L. Klerman, eds., *Contemporary Directions in Psychopathology*. New York: Guilford.

Millon, T. (1987a). On the genesis and prevalence of the borderline personality disorder: A social learning thesis. *Journal of Personality Disorders, 1*, 354–372.

Millon, T. (1987b). On the nature of taxonomy in psychopathology. In C. Last and M. Hersen, eds., *Issues in Diagnostic Research*. New York: Plenum.

Millon, T. (1988) Personologic psychotherapy: Ten commandments for a post eclectic approach to integrative treatment. *Psychotherapy, 25*, 209–219.

Millon, T. (in press, a). *Millon personality type questionnaire, manual*. Minneapolis: National Computer Systems.

Millon, T. (in press, b). Toward a normal personology: An evolutionary perspective. In D. Offer and M. Sabshin, eds., *Normality: Context and Theory*. New York: Basic Books.

Millon, T.; Tringone, R.; Green, C. J.; Sandberg, M.; et al (in press, c). *Millon personality diagnostic checklist, manual*. Minneapolis: National Computer Systems.

Mischel, W. (1984). Convergences and challenges in the search for consistency. *American Psychologist, 39*, 351–364.

Moruzzi, G., and Magoun, H. (1949). Brain stem reticular formation and activation of the EEG. *Electroencephalography and Clinical Neurophysiology, 1*, 455–473.

Murphy, G. (1947). *Personality: A biosocial approach to origins and structures*. New York: Harper.

Murray, H. A., ed. (1938). *Explorations in personality*. New York: Oxford University Press.

Murray, H. A. (1952). Toward a classification of interactions. In T. Parsons and E. Shiels, ed., *Toward a General Theory of Action*. Cambridge: Harvard University Press.

Murray, H. A. (1959). Preparations for the scaffold of a comprehensive system. In S. Koch, ed., *Psychology: A Study of a Science* (vol. 3). New York: McGraw-Hill.

Nebylitsyn, V. D., ed. (1969). *Problems of differential psychophysiology* (vol. 6). Moscow: Prosveshcheniye.

Nowlis, V., and Nowlis, H. H. (1956). The description and analysis of mood. *Annals of the New York Academy of Sciences, 65*, 345–355.

Olds, J. and Milner, P. (1954). Positive reinforcement produced by the electrical stimulation of septal region and other regions of rat brain. *Journal of Comparative and Physiological Psychology. 47*, 419–427.

Papez, J. (1937). A proposed mechanism of emotion. *Archives of Neurology and Psychiatry, 38*, 725–743.

Pavlov, I. (1927). *Conditioned reflexes.* Oxford, England: Oxford University Press.

Plutchik, R. and Conte, H. R. (1985). Quantitative assessment of personality disorders. In J. O. Cavenar, ed., *Psychiatry* (vol. I). Philadelphia: Lippincott.

Pribram, K. (1962). Interrelations of psychology and the neurological disciplines. In S. Koch, ed., *Psychology: A Study of a Science.* New York: McGraw-Hill.

Prigogine, I. (1972). Thermodynamics of evolution. *Physics Today, 25*, 23–28, 38–44.

Prigogine, I. (1976). Order through fluctuation: Self-organization and social system. In E. Jantsch and C. Waddington, eds., *Evolution and Consciousness.* Reading, MA: Addison-Wesley.

Quine, W. V. O. (1961). *From a logical point of view.* (2nd ed.) New York: Harper & Row.

Quine, W. V. O. (1977). Natural kinds. In S. P. Schwartz, ed. *Naming, Necessity and Natural Groups.* Ithaca: Cornell University Press.

Rapaport, D. (1953). Some metapsychological considerations concerning activity and passivity. In M. M. Gill (Ed.) *The Collected Papers of David Rapaport* (1967). New York: Basic Books.

Rapaport, D. (1959). The structure of psychoanalytic theory: A systematizing attempt. In S. Kock (Ed.) *Psychology: A Study of a science.* New York: McGraw-Hill.

Redmond, D.; Maas, J.; and Kling, A. (1971). Social behavior of monkeys selectively depleted of monoamines. *Science, 174*, 428–431.

Rotter, J. B. (1966). Generalized expectancies for internal versus external control of reinforcement. *Psychological Monographs, 80*, No. 1 (Whole No 609).

Rubin, J.; Provenzano, F.; and Luria, Z. (1974). The eye of the beholder: Parents' views of the sex of the newborn. *American Journal of Orthopsychiatry, 44*, 512–519.

Rushton, J. P. (1984). Sociobiology: Toward a theory of individual and group differences in personality and social behavior. In J. R. Royce and L. P. Moos, eds., *Annals of Theoretical Psychology* (vol. 2). New York: Plenum.

Rushton, J. P. (1985). Differential K theory: The sociobiology of individual and group differences. *Personality and Individual Differences*, 6, 441–452.

Russell, J. A. (1980). A circumplex model of affect. *Journal of Personality and Social Psychology*, 39, 1161–1178.

Russell, J. A., and Mehrabian, A. (1974). Distinguishing anger and anxiety in terms of emotional response factors. *Journal of Consulting and Clinical Psychology*, 42, 79–83.

Russell, J. A., and Mehrabian, A. (1977). Evidence for a three-factor theory of emotions. *Journal of Research in Personality*, 11, 273–294.

Russell, J. A., and Pratt, G. (1980). A description of the affective quality attributed to environments. *Journal of Personality and Social Psychology*, 38, 311–322.

Sage, A., and Hoffman, M. L. (1976). Empathic distress in newborns. *Developmental Psychology*, 12, 175–176.

Schafer, R. (1968). On the theoretical and technical conceptualization of activity and passivity:. *The Psychoanalytic Quarterly*, 37, 173–198.

Schneirla, T. C. (1959). An evolutionary and developmental theory of biphasic processes underlying approach and withdrawal. In M. R. Jones, ed., *Nebraska Symposium on Motivation*. Lincoln: University of Nebraska.

Schlosberg, H. (1952). The description of facial expressions in terms of two dimensions. *Journal of Experimental Psychology*, 44, 229–237.

Schrodinger, E. (1944). *What Is Life?* Cambridge: Cambridge University Press.

Sellars, W. (1963). *Science, perception and reality*. New York: Humanities Press.

Sjobring, H. (1973). Personality structure and development: A model and its application. *Acta Psychiatrica Scandinavica*, 244, 1–204.

Skinner, B. F. (1938). *The behavior of organisms; An experimental analysis*. New York: Appleton.

Skinner, B. F. (1953). *Science and human behavior.* New York: Macmillan.

Skutch, A. (1985). *Life ascending.* Austin: University of Texas Press.

Smith, E. E., and Medin, D. L. (1981). *Categories and concepts.* Cambridge, MA: Harvard University Press.

Spencer, H. (1870). *The principles of psychology.* London: Williams and Norgate.

Spinoza, B. de (1677/1986). *Ethics: On the correction of understanding.* London: Dent.

Steklis, H., and Kling, A. (1985). Neurobiology of affiliation in primates. In M. Reite and T. Fields, eds., *The Psychobiology of Attachment and Separation.* New York: Academic Press.

Strelau, J. (1983). *Temperament personality activity.* New York: Academic Press.

Szasz, T. S. (1975). *Pleasure and Pain.* New York: Basic Books.

Tellegen, A. (1985). Structures of mood and personality and relevance to assessing anxiety, with an emphasis on self-report. In A. H. Tuma and J. Maser, eds., *Anxiety and the Anxiety Disorders.* Hillsdale, NJ: Erlbaum.

Teplov, B. M. (1961). *Problems of Individuals Differences* (vol. 2). Moscow: RSFSR Academy of Pedagogical Sciences.

Thom, R. (1972). *Structural stability and morphogenesis.* Reading, MA: Benjamin.

Thorndike, E. L. (1905). *The elements of psychology.* New York: Seiler.

Thorndike, E. L. (1908). A pragmatic substitute for free will. In *Essays Philosophical and Psychological in Honor of William James.* New York: Longmans, Green.

Thorndike, E. L. (1932). *The fundamentals of learning.* New York: Teachers College.

Tolman, E. C. (1932). *Purposive behavior in animals and man.* New York: Appleton.

Tolstoy, L. (1903). *Reminiscences.* Moscow: Birynkov-Sytin.

Trivers, R. L. (1971). The evolution of reciprocal altruism. *Quarterly Review of Biology, 46,* 35–57.

Trivers, R. L. (1974). Parental investment and sexual selection. In B. Campbell, ed., *Sexual Selection and the Descent of Man 1871–1971.* Chicago: Aldine.

Tryon, E. (1973). Vacuum genesis. *Nature. 246*, 396–401.

Wachtel, P. (1977). *Psychoanalysis and behavior therapy: Toward an interpretation*. New York: Basic Books.

Watson, D., and Tellegen, A. (1984). Toward a consensual structure of mood. Unpublished manuscript. University of Minnesota.

White, R. W. (1959). Motivation reconsidered: The concept of competence. *Psychological Review, 66*, 297–323.

Wiggins, J. S. (1982). Circumplex models of interpersonal behavior in clinical psychology. In P. C. Kendall and J. N. Butcher, eds., *Handbook of Research Methods in Clinical Psychology*. New York: Wiley.

Wilson, E. O. (1975). *Sociobiology: The new synthesis*. Cambridge: Harvard University Press.

Wilson, E. O. (1978). *On human nature*. Cambridge: Harvard University Press.

Witkin, H. A., et al (1954). *Personality through perception*. New York: Harper & Row.

Witkin, H. A., and Goodenough, D. R. (1977). Field dependence and interpersonal behavior. *Psychological Bulletin, 84*, 661–689.

Yalom, I. D. (1986). *The theory and practice of group psychotherapy*. 3rd ed. New York: Basic Books.

Zevon, M. A., and Tellegen, A. (1982). The structure of mood change: An idiographic/nomothetic analysis. *Journal of Personality and Social Psychology, 43*, 111–122.

Zuckerman, M. (1979). *Sensation seeking: Beyond the optimal level of arousal*. Hillsdale, NJ: Erlbaum.

Author Index

Subject Index